Let's Do Fingerplays

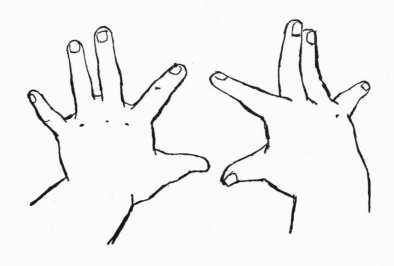

Let's
Do
Fingerplays

by **MARION GRAYSON**

Illustrated by **NANCY WEYL**

 ROBERT B. LUCE, INC.
Washington

LET'S DO FINGERPLAYS

PUBLISHED SIMULTANEOUSLY IN THE DOMINION OF CANADA

Seventh Printing, August 1973

LIBRARY OF CONGRESS CATALOG CARD NUMBER: 62-10217

MANUFACTURED IN THE UNITED STATES OF AMERICA

VAN REES PRESS • NEW YORK

TO ALL THOSE PEOPLE, BIG AND SMALL,
WHO HAD A HAND IN CREATING THIS BOOK.

Foreword

Fingerplays have been a part of children's literature for years. In fact, they have been the child's introduction to language and fun and companionship with older members of the family. Who of us does not recall with fond memories "This Little Pig Went to Market," or "Here Is the Church, Here Is the Steeple."

Marion Grayson has worked diligently for years gathering this collection. As a teacher and mother, she has had ample opportunity to test the appeal of these fingerplays in school and at home. Their everyday use has proved most popular with both preschool and kindergarten children, and they have been greatly enjoyed by early elementary school youngsters as well. Not only are the words, actions and expressions in fingerplays enjoyed by the individual child, but they have a special appeal to groups of young children. Their special appeal is often found to be particularly useful to teachers in gaining the attention of the group.

Mrs. Grayson has given excellent suggestions for getting the full dramatic effect from these fingerplays; however, she does not intend to discourage the use of original ideas. Sometimes, the children may modify a direction in the fingering, or may even change a word or line to suit the occasion. This makes the rhyme even more interesting to the youngster, for the rhyme becomes personal.

Books of fingerplays have been few and far between, and teachers and mothers, particularly, have been forced to tax their memories for fingerplays where a ready guide would be most acceptable.

This compilation of fingerplays includes the best of the old and a wide variety of delightful originals by the author. Together, they offer convincing proof that the author not only knows and understands young children but that she also has keen insight into the things which bring them fun and happiness.

Doris Erwin Hawkins, Consultant
National Child Research Center
Washington, D.C.

Acknowledgments

Grateful acknowledgment is made to the following for their permission to use their rhymes in this collection of fingerplays:

Broodmoor Press, Nashville, Tenn., for: "Helpfulness," and "The Window" by Aurora Medford Shumate, in *First Year Daily Vacation Bible School* textbook, by Aurora Medford Shumate; Harcourt, Brace and World, New York, for: "Jonathan Bing," by Beatrice Curtis Brown in *Rainbow in the Sky* by Louis Untermeyer. Pub. 1935; Harper & Brothers, New York, for "The Mitten Song," and "My Zipper Suit" by Mary Louise Allen from *Pocketful of Rhymes,* and found in *Very Young Verses for Very Young Children* by Barbara Peck Geismer and Antoinette Brown Suter, published by The Macmillan Co., New York, 1941; The Macmillan Co., New York, for: "Little Turtle" by Vachel Lindsay. Reprinted by permission of the publisher from *Johnny Appleseed and Other Poems,* by Vachel Lindsay. Copyright The Macmillan Co., and Copyright 1948 by Elizabeth C. Lindsay; Prentice-Hall, Inc., Englewood Cliffs, N. J., for: "The Stilt Man" by Gladys Andrews, from Gladys Andrews, *Creative Rhythmic Movement for Children,* Copyright 1954, Prentice-Hall, Inc., Englewood Cliffs, N. J., reprinted by permission; G. Schirmer & Co., New York, for: "When a Little Chicken Drinks" by Neidlinger from *Small Songs for Small Singers.* Pub. 1945. Copyright 1907, 1935 by G. Schirmer. Used by permission; Whitman & Co., Chicago, for: "Ten Little Fishes" by Florence Gillette Sumner and "Said This Little Fairy" by Maud Burnham from *Let's Play with Fingers,* by Maud Burnham. Pub. 1948; Marjorie Best Johnson for: "Come Follow Me," "Doggie's Tail," and "Open, Close Them"; Margaret A. Stant, for: "My Rabbit" and "The Alligator"; Jennie D. Siry for words to the songs: "The Windshield Wipers," Copyright 1959 and "The Metronome Song," Copyright 1960.

In some cases where poems have not been acknowledged, we have searched diligently to find sources and obtain permission to use the poems, but without success.

Contents

SECTION	SOURCE	PAGE
THE CHILD FROM TOP TO TOE		
Ten Fingers	Unknown	3
Busy Fingers	Unknown	3
Tommy Thumb	Traditional	4
Thumbkin, Pointer	Unknown	4
Little Fingers	French Folk Song	4
Fee, Fie, Foe, Fum	Unknown	5
Mister Thumb	Unknown	5
Where Is Thumbkin?	Unknown	6
Thumbkin Says "I'll Dance"	Unknown	8
Right Hand, Left Hand	Unknown	9
Come Follow Me	Marjorie Best Johnson	9
Clap Your Hands	Marion F. Grayson	10
Point to the Right	Marion F. Grayson	11
Five Fingers	Unknown	11
Eye Winker	Nursery Rhyme	11
My Hands	Unknown	12
Two Little Hands	Unknown	12
Knock at the Door	Nursery Rhyme	13
Hands on Shoulders	Unknown	13
This Is the Circle That Is My Head	Unknown	14
DRESSING UP		
Dressing	Marion F. Grayson	16
Hair Ribbons	Mary Louise Allen	17
My Hat	Unknown	17
Feather in My Hat	Marion F. Grayson	17
Cobbler, Cobbler	Mother Goose—adapted	18
Mittens	Marion F. Grayson	18
Old Shoes, New Shoes	Unknown	18
My Zipper Suit	Mary Louise Allen	18
Shiny Shoes	Unknown	19
Five Little Girls	Marion F. Grayson	20
The Mitten Song	Mary Louise Allen	20

SECTION	SOURCE	PAGE

THINGS THAT GO

An Airplane	Unknown	22
The Train	Unknown	22
Down by the Station	Traditional	22
The Big Train	Unknown	22
Choo-Choo Train	Unknown	23
Big Hill	Unknown	23
The Windshield Wipers	Jennie D. Siry	24
Auto, Auto	Marion F. Grayson	24
Driving down the Street	Marion F. Grayson	25
The Bus	Unknown	25
The Steam Shovel	Marion F. Grayson	26
The Boats	Unknown	26
Row, Row, Row Your Boat	Traditional	26
Clocks	Traditional	27
The Top	Marion F. Grayson	27
I Have a Little Watch	Marion F. Grayson	27
The Metronome Song	Jennie D. Siry	28

ANIMAL ANTICS

Dog Went to Dover	Nursery Rhyme—adapted	30
This Little Doggie	Unknown	30
Doggie's Tail	Marjorie Best Johnson	30
Little Mousie	Unknown	30
Hickory, Dickory, Dock	Nursery Rhyme	31
Eensy, Weensy Spider	Nursery Rhyme	31
This Little Pig	Nursery Rhyme	32
Kitten Is Hiding	Unknown	32
The Alligator	Margaret Stant	32
My Turtle	Unknown	32
There Was a Little Turtle	Vachel Lindsay	33
My Rabbit	Margaret Stant	34
The Bear Went over the Mountain	Traditional	34
This Little Squirrel	Unknown	35
Golden Fishes	Unknown	35
Once I Saw a Bunny	Unknown	35
When a Little Chicken Drinks	Niedlinger	36
Bunny	Unknown	36
Five Little Ducks	Unknown	36
Snail Song	Unknown	37
Little Bird	Unknown	37
Little Robin Redbreast	Nursery Rhyme	37
This Little Calf	Unknown	38

SECTION	SOURCE	PAGE

THE FAMILY

Good Little Mother	Traditional	40
Grandma's Spectacles	Unknown	41
The Family	Traditional	41
This Is the Mother	Traditional	41
Kitty, Kitty	Traditional	42
Chickens	Unknown	42
Sleepy Fingers	Unknown	43
Bunnies' Bedtime	Unknown	43
Rock-a-Bye Baby, Thy Cradle Is Green	Nursery Rhyme	44

THE WORLD OUTDOORS

My Garden	Unknown	46
Pitter-Pat	Unknown	46
Raindrops	Marion F. Grayson	47
Whirling Leaves	Unknown	47
October	Unknown	47
Leaves	Unknown	47
Falling Leaves	Marion F. Grayson	47
Snowflakes	Unknown	48
Snow Man	Unknown	48
Apples	Unknown	48

BIG PEOPLE, LITTLE PEOPLE

People	Marion F. Grayson	50
The Stilt Man	Florence Burns	50
Aiken Drum	Nursery Rhyme	51
Jack and Jill	Nursery Rhyme—adapted	52
Rock-a-Bye Baby	Nursery Rhyme	52
Here Is the Church	Nursery Rhyme	52
Ten Little Firemen	Unknown	53
King of France	Nursery Rhyme—adapted	53
Playmates	Unknown	54
Sing a Song of Sixpence	Nursery Rhyme	55
Warm Hands	Traditional	55
Jack-in-the-Box	Unknown	55
Jonathan Bing	Beatrice Curtis Brown	56
Snip, Snip, Snip, Snippety	Marion F. Grayson	57
Thieken Man	Old Norwegian Fingerplay	57
Creeping Indians	Unknown	57
Said This Little Fairy	Maude Burnham	57
Shiver and Quiver	Marion F. Grayson	58

SECTION	SOURCE	PAGE

COUNTING AND COUNTING OUT

Catching a Fish	Nursery Rhyme—adapted	60
Chickadees	Unknown	60
Five Little Indians	Nursery Rhyme—adapted	61
Frogs	Unknown	62
Five Little Froggies	Unknown	62
Five Little Squirrels	Unknown	63
Five Little Ants	Florence Gillette Sumner	63
I Caught a Hare	Nursery Rhyme	64
Five Little Kittens	Unknown	64
Great Big Ball	Unknown	64
Grasshoppers	Unknown	65
One, Two, Buckle My Shoe	Nursery Rhyme	66
Hot Cross Buns	Nursery Rhyme	66
Telegraph Poles	Unknown	66
Soldiers	Unknown	66
Johnny's Hammer	Unknown	67
This Old Man	Traditional	68
Ten Little Indians	Traditional	69
Ten Little Men	Unknown	70
One for the Money	Nursery Rhyme	70
Tennessee	Traditional	70
Two Little Houses	Unknown	70
Counting Out	Mother Goose	71
Two Little Ducks	Unknown	71
Two Mother Pigs	Unknown	72
Bumblebee	Unknown	73
Eeny, Meeny, Miney, Mo	Mother Goose	73
Two Little Blackbirds	Nursery Rhyme	73
Mary at the Cottage Door	Mother Goose	74
Tee-Taw-Buck	Mother Goose	74
Ten Little Fishes	Florence Gillette Sumner	74

AROUND THE HOUSE

The House	Unknown	76
Up, Up	Nursery Rhyme—adapted	76
Who Feels Happy?	Unknown	76
Swinging	Unknown	77
The Seesaw	Marion F. Grayson	78
The Window	Aurora Medford Shumate	78
Wind the Bobbin	Danish Folk Song	78
Up the Steps We Go	Unknown	78
Open, Close Them	Marjorie Best Johnson	79
Up a Step	Unknown	79
Pat-a-Cake	Nursery Rhyme	80

SECTION	SOURCE	PAGE
Good Morning	Unknown	80
I Shut the Door	Unknown	81
The Very Nicest Place	Unknown	81
Tap at the Door	Unknown	81
Helpfulness	Aurora Medford Shumate	82
The Teapot	Unknown	82
The Little Wash Bench	Unknown	83
Here's a Cup	Unknown	83
We Wash Our Shirt	Marion F. Grayson	84

NOISE MAKERS

The Finger Band	Maude Burnham	86
I Am a Fine Musician	Traditional	87
Hammering	Marion F. Grayson	88
Peas Porridge	Nursery Rhyme	88
Shake, Shake, Knock, Knock	Unknown	88
Ten Little Soldiers	Unknown	88
Pound Goes the Hammer	Unknown	89
Balloons	Unknown	89
Let Your Hands Clap	Unknown	90
Indians	Unknown	90

HOLIDAYS AND SPECIAL OCCASIONS

Christmas Is A-Coming	Nursery Rhyme	92
Christmas Bells	Marion F. Grayson	92
Santa Claus	Unknown	92
Christmas Tree	Traditional	93
Little Jack Horner	Nursery Rhyme	94
Here Is the Chimney	Unknown	94
Our Table	Unknown	94
I've a Jack-o'-Lantern	Unknown	95
Halloween Witches	Unknown	95
Jack-o'-Lanterns	Unknown	95
Witch's Cat	Unknown	96
My Pumpkin	Unknown	97
Very Nice Jack-o'-Lantern	Unknown	97
The Friendly Ghost	Marion F. Grayson	97
Scary Eyes	Unknown	97
Coal-Black Cat	Unknown	98
Witch	Unknown	98
Make A Valentine	Marion F. Grayson	99
Valentine's Good Morning	Traditional	99
Valentine for You	Unknown	99
The Circus	Marion F. Grayson	100
Five Years Old	Mary Louise Allen	101
Bedtime	Unknown	101

Introduction

LET'S DO FINGERPLAYS is a collection for mothers and teachers of the many, many fingerplays which have been handed down to us for generations, mostly by word of mouth, as well as the newer ones which have emanated from our more modern way of living.

The action, repetition, rhythm, and dramatization in these rhymes will entrance the toddler as well as the early elementary school child, because they are fun to do.

Nursery, kindergarten, and elementary schoolteachers are finding fingerplays an invaluable aid to memory training and the teaching of early number concepts. For this reason, many fingerplays which teach children to count have been included.

Fingerplays are another means of satisfying the hunger for "Tell me a story." They are introductions to "story time"; they quiet children before meal or nap time, or any other change in activity. Children find them fascinating because they themselves participate immediately in telling the story by "making" the picture, rather than by "seeing" it.

It is easy to do these fingerplays, for simple instructions follow right along with each line of verse. It is important to remember, however, that if the narrator is facing the children, she must use her LEFT hand whenever the rhyme calls for the RIGHT, because children try to imitate *exactly*, and the narrator's *left* will be the children's *right*. Also, these rhymes must be spoken slowly and distinctly as the children's reaction time is considerably slower than the adults'—the younger the children, the more slowly they react.

Grateful appreciation is due the many mothers and teachers whose hearts and hands have imbued these pages: To Doris Erwin Hawkins, Consultant and formerly Director of the National Child Research Center, Washington, D.C., for her wise counseling and criticism; to Jennie Siry, Music Supervisor at the Center, for her interest and suggestions; and especially to my long-time co-worker, Marjorie Best Johnson, for her invaluable assistance on research, and without whom I might still be lost in the stacks of the Library of Congress. Warm thanks are also due the children on Twentieth Street, Northwest, who were able, if wide-eyed critics.

MARION F. GRAYSON

Washington, D.C.
August, 1962

The Child
from
Top to Toe

Ten Fingers

I have ten little fingers
> *(Follow action as rhyme indicates.)*

And they all belong to me.
I can make them do things.
Would you like to see?
I can shut them up tight
Or open them wide.
I can put them together
Or make them all hide.
I can make them jump high,
I can make them jump low,
I can fold them quietly
And hold them just so.

Busy Fingers

This is the way my fingers stand, fingers stand, fingers stand,
> *(Follow action as rhyme indicates.)*

This is the way my fingers stand, so early in the morning.
This is the way they dance about, dance about, dance about,
This is the way they dance about, so early in the morning.
This is the way I fold my hands, fold my hands, fold my hands,
This is the way I fold my hands, so early in the morning.
This is the way they go to rest, go to rest, go to rest,
This is the way they go to rest, so early in the morning.
> *(Cup hands loosely, palms up and place in lap.)*

Tommy Thumb

This is little Tommy Thumb,
(Point to each finger in turn.)
Round and smooth as any plum
This is busy Peter Pointer,
Surely he's a double-jointer.
This is mighty Toby Tall,
He's the biggest one of all.
This is dainty Reuben Ring,
He's too fine for anything.
And this little wee one maybe,
Is the pretty Finger Baby!

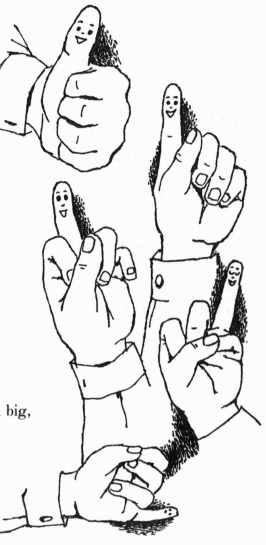

Thumbkin, Pointer

Thumbkin, Pointer, Middleman big,
(Point to each finger in turn.
Then roll hands at end.)
Silly Man, Wee Man, rig-a-jig.

Little Fingers

They do so, so, so,
(Hold up hands. Extend fingers and wiggle them.)
Little fingers, little fingers,
They do so, so, so,
(Repeat first instruction.)
Turn three times and away they go.
(Turn hands away from each other three times;
hide behind back.)

Fee, Fie, Foe, Fum

Fee, fie, fo, fum,
(Point to little finger for "fee," etc.)

See my finger,
(Point to finger before thumb.)

See my thumb.
(Point to thumb.)

Fee, fie, fo, fum,
(Point to fingers.)

Finger's gone,
(Hide finger in hand.)

So is thumb.
(Hide thumb.)

Mister Thumb

Mister Thumb, Mister Thumb, where are you?
(Make fists.)

Here I am, here I am. How do you do?
(Extend thumbs and wiggle them.)

Peter Pointer, Peter Pointer, where are you?

Here I am. Here I am. How do you do?
(Extend each pair of fingers as called for.)

Ruby Ring, Ruby Ring, where are you?

Here I am. Here I am. How do you do?

Baby Small, Baby Small, where are you?

Here I am, here I am. How do you do?

Fingers all, fingers all, where are you?

Here we are, here we are. How do you do?

Where Is Thumbkin?

Where is Thumbkin? Where is Thumbkin?
(Put hands behind back.)

Here I am. Here I am.
(Show one thumb; then the other.)

How are you this morning?
(Bend one thumb.)

Very well, I thank you.
(Bend other thumb.)

Run and play. Run and play.

Where is Pointer? Where is Pointer?

Here I am. Here I am.
(Show one index finger; then the other)

How are you this morning?
(Bend one index finger.)

Very well, I thank you.
(Bend other index finger.)

Run and play. Run and play.
(Put index fingers behind back.)

Where is Tall Man? Where is Tall Man?

Here I am. Here I am.
(Show one tall finger; then the other.)

How are you this morning?
(Bend one tall finger.)

Very well, I thank you.
(Bend other tall finger.)

Run and play. Run and play.
(Put tall fingers behind back.)

6

Where is Feeble Man? Where is Feeble Man?
Here I am. Here I am.
   (Show one ring finger; then the other.)
How are you this morning?
   (Bend one ring finger.)
Very well, I thank you.
   (Bend other ring finger.)
Run and play. Run and play.
   (Put ring fingers behind back.)

Where is Baby? Where is Baby?
Here I am. Here I am.
   (Show one baby finger; then the other.)
How are you this morning?
   (Bend one baby finger.)
Very well, I thank you.
   (Bend the other baby finger.)
Run and play. Run and play.
   (Put baby fingers behind back.)

Where are all the Men? Where are all the Men?
Here they are. Here they are.
   (Show all fingers on one hand; then the other.)
How are you this morning?
   (Bend fingers of one hand.)
Very well, we thank you.
   (Bend fingers of other hand.)
Run and play. Run and play.
   (Put hands behind back.)

Thumbkin Says "I'll Dance"

Thumbkin says, "I'll dance."
(Hold up hands, wiggle each pair of fingers, as rhyme indicates.)
Thumbkin says, "I'll sing."
Dance and sing, you merry little thing.
Thumbkin says, "I'll dance and sing."

Pointer says, "I'll dance."
Pointer says, "I'll sing."
Dance and sing, you merry little thing,
Pointer says, "I'll dance and sing."

Tall Man says, "I'll dance."
Tall Man says, "I'll sing."
Dance and sing, you merry little thing.
Tall Man says, "I'll dance and sing."

Ring Man says, "I'll dance."
Ring Man says, "I'll sing."
Dance and sing, you merry little thing.
Ring Man says, "I'll dance and sing."

Baby says, "I'll dance."
Baby says, "I'll sing."
Dance and sing, you merry little thing.
Baby says, "I'll dance and sing."

All the Men say they'll dance.
(Wiggle all the fingers.)
All the Men say they'll sing.
Dance and sing, you merry little things.
All the Men say they'll dance and sing.

Right Hand, Left Hand

This is my right hand,
(Follow action as rhyme indicates.)
I'll raise it up high.
This is my left hand.
I'll touch the sky.
Right hand, left hand,
Roll them around.
Left hand, right hand,
Pound, pound, pound.

Come Follow Me

Come follow, follow, follow,
(Beckon with finger.)
Come follow, follow me.
(Beckon.)
Come follow, follow, follow,
(Beckon.)
And here is where you'll be.
(Point to nose, or eyes, or shoulders, etc.)

Clap Your Hands

Clap your hands, clap your hands,
Clap them just like me.
(Action as indicated by rhyme.)

Touch your shoulders, touch your shoulders,
Touch them just like me.

Tap your knees, tap your knees,
Tap them just like me.

Shake your head, shake your head,
Shake it just like me.

Clap your hands, clap your hands,
Now let them quiet be.

10

Point to the Right

Point to the right of me,
> *(Use both arms and follow action slowly as rhyme indicates.)*

Point to the left of me,
Point up above me,
Point down below.
Right, left, up,
> *(Increase speed in pointing.)*

And down so slow.
> *(Decrease speed.)*

Eye Winker

Eye Winker,
> *(Point to eyes.)*

Tom Tinker,
> *(Point to ears.)*

Nose Smeller,
> *(Point to nose.)*

Mouth Eater,
> *(Point to mouth.)*

Chin Chopper,
> *(Tap chin.)*

Chin Chopper, Chin Chopper,
Chin Chopper, chin.

Five Fingers

Five fingers on this hand,
> *(Hold up one hand.)*

Five fingers on that;
> *(Hold up other hand.)*

A dear little nose,
> *(Point to nose.)*

A mouth like a rose,
> *(Point to mouth.)*

Two cheeks so tiny and fat.
> *(Point to each cheek.)*

Two eyes, two ears,
> *(Point to each.)*

And ten little toes;
> *(Point to toes.)*

That's the way the baby grows.

My Hands

My hands upon my head I place,
(Follow action as rhyme indicates.)
On my shoulders, on my face;
On my hips I place them, so.
Now I raise them up so high,
Make my fingers fairly fly.
Now I clap them, one, two, three,
Then I fold them silently.

Two Little Hands

Two little hands so soft and white.
(Show them.)
This is the left; this is the right.
(Indicate each.)
Five little fingers standing on each,
(Show fingers.)
So I can hold a plum or a peach.
(Curve fingers as if holding plum.)
But when I get as big as you,
(Point to child.)
I'll show you what these hands can do.
(Show hands.)

Knock at the Door

Knock at the door,
(Tap forehead.)

Peep in.
(Point to eyes.)

Lift up the latch,
(Tap end of nose.)

Walk in.
(Open mouth; hold finger near.)

Chin Chopper, Chin Chopper,
(Tap under chin.)

Chin Chopper, chin.

Hands on Shoulders

Hands on shoulders, hands on knees,
(Follow action as rhyme indicates.)
Hands behind you, if you please;
Touch your shoulders, now your nose,
Now your hair and now your toes;
Hands up high in the air,
Down at your sides and touch your hair;
Hands up high as before,
Now clap your hands, one, two, three, four.

This Is the Circle That Is My Head

This is the circle that is my head,
  (Make large circle with both hands.)
This is my mouth with which words are said,
  (Point to mouth.)
These are my eyes with which I see,
  (Point to eyes.)
This is my nose that's a part of me.
  (Point to nose.)
This is the hair that grows on my head,
  (Point to hair.)
This is my hat, all pretty and red,
  (Place hands on head, fingers pointed up and touching.)
This is the feather so bright and gay,
  (Extend index finger upward along side of head.)
Now I'm all ready for school today.

Dressing Up

Dressing

Children put your pants on, pants on, pants on;
Children put your pants on,—one, two, three.
   (Follow action as rhyme indicates.)

Children put your socks on, socks on, socks on;
Children put your socks on—one, two, three.
Children put your shoes on, shoes on, shoes on;
Children put your shoes on—one, two, three.
Children put your shirt on, shirt on, shirt on;
Children put your shirt on—one, two, three.
Children put your sweater on, sweater on, sweater on;
Children put your sweater on—one, two, three.

Children now are all dressed, all dressed, all dressed;
   (Clap hands.)
Children now are all dressed, let's go play!

Hair Ribbons

I'm three years old and like to wear
(Indicate three fingers.)

A bow of ribbon on my hair.
(Make a circle with thumb and index finger of each hand and join on top of head.)

Sometimes it's pink, sometimes it's blue.
I think it's pretty there, don't you?

My Hat

My hat, it has three corners,
(Join thumbs and index fingers and place on top of head.)

Three corners has my hat.
(Raise three fingers.)

If it did not have three corners,
(Raise three fingers and shake head.)

It would not be my hat.
(Join thumbs and index fingers and place on top of head.)

Feather in My Hat

If I'd put a feather in my hat,
(Hold index finger up alongside of head.)

I'd look like Yankee Doodle.
Now what do you think of that!

Cobbler, Cobbler

Cobbler, cobbler, mend my shoe,
(Hold one foot on other knee.)
Have it done by half-past two;
(Hammer shoe with fist.)
Stitch it up and stitch it down,
(Make sewing motions on shoe.)
Now nail the heel all around.
(Make hammering motions around shoe heel.)

Mittens

Slide your fingers into the wide part,
(Hold right hand forward, palm down, fingers together, thumb apart.)
Make your thumb stand alone and tall.
(Slide left hand over grouped fingers and then over thumb.)
When you put your mittens on,
You won't feel cold at all.

My Zipper Suit

My zipper suit is bunny brown,
(Point to clothes.)
The top zips up, the leg zips down.
(Draw fingers up as if pulling zipper; then down along legs.)
I wear it every day.
My daddy brought it out from town.
Zip it up, zip it down,
(Zip up, zip down.)
And hurry out to play.

Old Shoes, New Shoes

Old shoes, new shoes,
(Point to child's shoes; first one, then the other.)
Black and brown and red shoes,
One, two, three, four,
(Show four fingers.)
Tapping softly on the floor.
(Tap fingers on floor.)

Shiny Shoes

First I loosen mud and dirt,
(Hold hand in front for shoe; brush off with other.)

My shoes I then rub clean,
(Rub shoe with palm of other hand.)

For shoes in such a dreadful sight
(Hide shoe behind back for moment, then return.)

Never should be seen.
Next I spread the polish on,
*(Join thumb and index finger of one hand to make
polish spreader and pretend to coat shoe.)*

And then I let it dry.
I brush and brush, and brush, and brush,
(Make fist and brush shoe vigorously.)

How those shoes shine! Oh, my!
(Extend hand and admire.)

Five Little Girls

Five little girls woke up in their beds.
> *(Curl fingers of one hand loosely in palm.)*

This little girl jumped right out of bed,
> *(Starting with thumb, let each finger pop up for one girl.)*

This little girl shook her curly head,
This little girl washed her sleepy face,
This little girl got all her clothes in place,
This little girl put on her shoes and socks,
And they all ran down to breakfast when the time was eight o'clock.
> *(All fingers run behind back.)*

The Mitten Song

"Thumb in the thumb place,
> *(Hold one hand up, fingers together, thumb apart; point to thumb and then to fingers.)*

Fingers all together!"
This is the song we sing in mitten weather,
When it's cold
> *(Rub hands together.)*

It doesn't matter whether
Mittens are wool
> *(Hold two hands up, fingers together, thumbs apart.)*

Or made of finest leather.
This is the song we sing in mitten weather;
"Thumb in the thumb place,
> *(Hold one hand up, fingers together, thumb apart; point to thumb and then to fingers.)*

Fingers all together!"

Things That
Go

An Airplane

If I had an airplane,
*(Extend right hand in front of body horizontally,
palm opened flat, facing down.)*

Zum, zum, zum,
I would fly to Mexico,
(Fly hand through air.)

Wave my hand and off I'd go.
(Wave to people.)

If I had an airplane,
(Repeat first instruction.)

Zum, zum, zum.

The Train

Choo, choo, choo,
(Slide hands together.)

The train runs down the track.
(Run fingers down arm.)

Choo, choo, choo,
(Slide hands together.)

And then it runs right back.
(Run fingers up arm.)

Down by the Station

Down by the station, early in the morning,
(Tap legs or clap hands.)

Do you see the engines standing in a row?
Do you see the engineer pull the big whistle?
(Close fist, raise high, pull downward.)

Toot, toot, choo, choo, off we go.
(Blow for "toot," slide palms together for "choo.")

The Big Train

The great big train goes up the track
*(Hold index and third finger close together,
and move up other arm.)*

And says *Whoo-oo* * and then goes back.
(Stop at shoulder. Blow whistle and then go back.)

* Child may choose different things for the train to say.

Choo-Choo Train

This is a choo-choo train
  (Bend arms at elbows.)
Puffing down the track.
  (Rotate forearms in rhythm.)
Now it's going forward,
  *(Push arms forward; continue
    rotating motion.)*
Now it's going back.
  *(Pull arms back; continue rotating
    motion.)*

Now the bell is ringing,
  (Pull bell cord with closed fist.)
Now the whistle blows.
  (Hold fist near mouth and blow.)
What a lot of noise it makes
  (Cover ears with hands.)
Everywhere it goes.
  (Stretch out arms.)

Big Hill

Here's a great big hill
  (Extend arm sideways to form hill.)
With snow all over the side.
Let's take our sleds
  (Place other hand on opposite shoulder, palm down.)
And down the hill we'll slide.
  (Slide hand down arm.)

The Windshield Wipers

The windshield wipers on our car are busy in the rain,
  *(Hold up both hands, palms turned outward and
  move them from side to side.)*
They swing, and swing, clup-clup-clup-clup,
Then back and forth again.

But when our car climbs up a hill,
  (Move hands more slowly.)
The wipers go so slow.
They swing and swing, clu-up-clu-up,
And sometimes stop! You know.
  (Hands stand still.)

When we coast down the other side,
  (Move hands more rapidly.)
The wipers go so fast.
They swing and swing, clup-cluppety, clup-cluppety,
  (Move hands very fast.)
As we go whizzing past.

Auto, Auto

Auto, auto, may I have a ride?
  *(Make fists, thumbs up. One thumb moves
  as if talking to other.)*
Yes, sir; yes, sir; step right inside.
  (Other thumb talks.)
Pour in the water,
  (Move first thumb as if pouring in water.)
Turn on the gas.
  (Move same thumb and index finger to turn switch.)
Chug-away, chug-away,
  (Pretend to hold steering wheel.)
But do not go too fast.

Driving down the Street

Let's drive our auto down the street,
*(Extend arms forward, make fists
and rotate arms to simulate steering.)*

Always looking straight ahead.
We'll have to stop when the light turns red.
(Hold arms still.)

Waiting, watching, through the windshield clean,
(Lean forward slightly and peer.)

We can go now; the light's turned green.
(Rotate arms again.)

The Bus

The wheels of the bus go round and round,
Round and round, round and round.
(Hold hands in front and roll one over the other.)
The wheels of the bus go round and round
Over the city streets.

The driver of the bus blows his horn. Beep-beep-beep,
Beep-beep-beep.
(Press thumb on fist.)
The driver of the bus blows his horn
Over the city streets.

The driver of the bus says, "Pay your fare,
Pay your fare, pay your fare."
(Extend hand as if receiving fare.)
The driver of the bus says, "Pay your fare,"
Over the city streets.

The people on the bus go bump, bump, bump;
Bump, bump, bump; bump, bump, bump;
(Jounce up and down.)
Over the city streets.

The Steam Shovel

The steam shovel scoop opens its mouth so wide;

*(Extend left hand in front, palm up,
fingers closed. Slowly open fingers.)*

Then scoops up the dirt and lays it aside.

*(Lower hand, "dig up dirt," move arm
to left and "dump it out.")*

The Boats

This is the way, all the long day,

*(Use one hand as boat and the other as bridge and
move hand back and forth under bridge.)*

The boats go sailing by,
To and fro, in a row,
Under the bridge so high.

Row, Row, Row Your Boat

Row, row, row your boat,

*(Fold arms high in front of chest, with elbows
extending out, and fisted hands meeting; reach
forward and pull back as if rowing.)*

Gently down the stream.
Merrily, merrily, merrily, merrily,
Life is but a dream.

(Repeat.)

Clocks

Big clocks make a sound like t-i-c-k, t-o-c-k,
t-i-c-k, t-o-c-k.

> *(Rest elbows on hips; extend forearms and index fingers up
> and move arms sideways slowly and rhythmically.)*

Small clocks make a sound like tick, tock, tick, tock.

> *(Move arms faster for second line.)*

And the very tiny clocks make a sound like tick, tock, tick, tock,

> *(Move still faster for last line.)*

Tick, tock, tick, tock, tick, tock, tick, tock, tick.

The Top

I have a top,

> *(Hold thumb and index finger of one hand
> together to make "top.")*

It spins and spins.

> *(Rotate top in open palm of other hand.)*

MM-mm-mm-mm.

> *(Hum.)*

It spins around

> *(Rotate top in open palm.)*

And soon it stops.

> *(Let top flop in palm of left hand.)*

MM-mm-mm-mm.

> *(Hum.)*

I Have a Little Watch

I have a little watch right here;

> *(Make circle with thumb and index finger for watch.)*

Hold it way up near your ear.

> *(Hold circle close to ear.)*

Hear it ticking, ticking fast?
It tells us when our playtime's past.

The Metronome Song

Tick, tick, tick, tick, says the metronome,
*(Hold left finger upright and move
from side to side.)*

When the weight is near the top,
*(Make circle with left thumb
and forefinger and raise hand.)*

It goes so slow it seems to stop!
*(Move finger from side to side
again, very slowly, and stop.)*

Tick, tick, tick, tick, says the metronome,
(Repeat first instruction.)

When the weight is way down low,
*(Make circle with left thumb and forefinger
and lower hand.)*

It swings so fast, just watch it go!
*(Move finger from side to side
very fast.)*

Animal Antics

Dog Went to Dover

Leg over leg
*(Hold arm forward and "step" fingers of other
hand toward arm.)*

As the dog went to Dover,
He came to a stile,
And jump—he went over.
(Jump fingers over arm.)

This Little Doggie

This little doggie ran away to play,
*(Hold up fingers of one hand;
point to each finger in turn.)*

This little doggie said, "I'll go too some day."
This little doggie began to dig and dig,
This little doggie danced a funny jig.
This little doggie cried, "Ki! Yi! Ki! Yi!
I wish I were big."

Doggie's Tail

A little doggie all brown and black,
*(Make fist with one hand; extend thumb and
index fingers touching each other for head.)*

Wore his tail curled on his back.
*(Curl other index finger and hold against
back of fist for tail.)*

Little Mousie

See the little mousie
(Put index and middle finger on thumb for "mouse.")

Creeping up the stair,
(Creep mouse slowly up other forearm, bent at elbow.)

Looking for a warm nest.
There—Oh! There.
(Let mouse spring into elbow corner.)

Hickory, Dickory, Dock

Hickory, dickory, dock,
(Bend arm at elbow; hold up, palm open.)

The mouse ran up the clock,
(Run fingers up arm.)

The clock struck one,
(Point to "one o'clock.")

The mouse ran down,
(Run fingers down arm.)

Hickory, dickory, dock.

Eensy, Weensy Spider

Eensy, weensy spider
*(Let opposite thumbs and index fingers
climb up each other.)*

Climbed up the waterspout.

Down came the rain
(Let hands sweep down and open wide.)

And washed the spider out.

Out came the sun
(Form circle over head with arms.)

And dried up all the rain.

So the eensy, weensy spider,
*(Let opposite thumbs and fingers
climb up each other again.)*

Climbed up the spout again.

Kitten Is Hiding

A kitten is hiding under a chair.
  (Hide one thumb under other hand.)
I looked and looked for her everywhere.
  (Peer about.)
Under the table and under the bed;
  (Pretend to look.)
I looked in the corner, and when I said,
"Come, Kitty, come, Kitty, here's milk for you."
  (Cup hands to make dish and extend.)
Kitty came running and calling, "Mew, mew."
  (Run fingers up arm.)

This Little Pig

This little pig went to market,
  (Point to each finger in turn.)
This little pig stayed home,
This little pig had roast beef,
This little pig had none,
This little pig cried, "Wee, wee, wee,"
  (Run hand behind back.)
All the way home!

The Alligator

The alligator likes to swim.
  *(Two hands flat, one on top of the
  other.)*
Sometimes his mouth opens wide,
  (Hands open and shut.)
But when he sees me on the shore,
  (Hands go between legs.)
Down under the water he'll hide.

My Turtle

This is my turtle,
  (Make fist; extend thumb.)
He lives in a shell.
  (Hide thumb in fist.)
He likes his home very well.
He pokes his head out when he wants to eat.
  (Extend thumb.)
And pulls it back in when he wants to sleep.
  (Hide thumb in fist.)

32

There Was a Little Turtle

There was a little turtle,
(Make small circle with hands.)

He lived in a box,
(Make box with both hands.)

He swam in a puddle,
(Wiggle hands.)

He climbed on the rocks.
(Climb fingers of one hand up over other.)

He snapped at a mosquito,
(Clap hands.)

He snapped at a flea,
(Clap hands.)

He snapped at a minnow,
(Clap hands.)

He snapped at me.
(Point to self.)

He caught the mosquito,
*(Hold hands up, palm facing forward;
quickly bend fingers shut.)*

He caught the flea,
*(Hold hands up, palm facing forward;
quickly bend fingers shut.)*

He caught the minnow,
*(Hold hands up, palm facing forward;
quickly bend fingers shut.)*

But he didn't catch me.
(Bend fingers only half way shut.)

33

My Rabbit

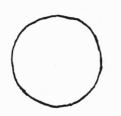

My rabbit has two big ears
(Hold up index and middle fingers for ears.)

And a funny little nose.
(Join other three fingers for nose.)

He likes to nibble carrots,
(Move thumb away from other two fingers.)

And he hops wherever he goes.
(Move whole hand jerkily.)

The Bear Went over the Mountain

The bear went over the mountain,
(Extend forearm, close and drop fist.)

The bear went over the mountain,
(Slowly creep fingers of other hand up over first hand to wrist.)

The bear went over the mountain,
To see what he could see.
(Hold above position.)

And what do you think he saw?
And what do you think he saw?

The other side of the mountain,
The other side of the mountain,
The other side of the mountain,
Is all that he did see!

So the bear went down the mountain,
(Creep fingers down sloping forearm.)

So the bear went down the mountain,
So the bear went down the mountain.
Very hap-pi-ly.

This Little Squirrel

This little squirrel said, "Let's run and play."
(Point to each finger in turn.)

This little squirrel said, "Let's hunt nuts today."
This little squirrel said, "Yes, nuts are good."
This little squirrel said, "Yes, they're our best food."
This little squirrel said, "Come climb this tree,
(Hold forearm up, hand open; run fingers of other hand to top fast, ending with thumb and forefinger making circle.)

And crack these nuts, one, two, three."
(Clap hands.)

Golden Fishes

Golden fishes swimming, floating,
(Hold palms of hands together and wiggle them around.)

Swimming, floating, all day long.

Once I Saw a Bunny

Once I saw a bunny
(Extend index and middle finger of one hand upward.)

And a green, green, cabbage head.
(Make fist with other hand.)

"I think I'll have some cabbage,"
The little bunny said.
So he nibbled and he nibbled,
(Make bobbing motion with finger and thumb of first hand.)

And he pricked his ears to say,
(Extend index and middle fingers upward.)

"Now I think it's time
I should be hopping on my way."
(Let hand hop away.)

35

When a Little Chicken Drinks

I think when a little chicken drinks
(Make loose fist, thumb and index touching, for chicken's head.)
He takes the water in his bill,
(Cup other hand, palm up and dip first fist into it.)
And then he holds his head way up
(Hold up first fist.)
So the water can run downhill.
(Draw other index finger down along first forearm.)

Bunny

Here is a bunny with ears so funny,
(Bend two fingers of one hand over on thumb.)
And here is his hole in the ground.
(Make a hole with other fist.)
When a noise he hears, he pricks up his ears
(Extend index and tall fingers of first hand, and then close them.)
And hops into his hole in the ground.
(Jump fingers into hole in other fist.)

Five Little Ducks

Five little ducks went in for a swim;
(Hold up hand; extend fingers.)
The first little duck put his head in.
(Point to each finger in turn.)
The second little duck put his head back;
The third little duck said, "Quack, quack, quack."
The fourth little duck with his tiny brother,
Went for a walk with his father and mother.
("Walk" fingers up opposite arm.)

Snail Song

The snail is so slow, the snail is so slow,
(*Creep fist along arm very slowly in rhythm.*)
He creeps and creeps along.
And as he does he sings his song;
The snail is so-o-o s-l-o-w.

Little Bird

I saw a little bird go hop, hop, hop.
(*Rest index and tall fingers on thumb;
make bobbing motion from wrist.*)

I told the little bird to stop, stop, stop.
(*Point each "stop" with index finger.*)

I went to the window to say, "How do you do?"
(*Extend hand as if to shake hands.*)

He wagged his little tail
(*Rest index and tall fingers on thumb; curl other index
finger and attach at back of hand.*)

And away he flew.
(*Fly fingers over head and behind back.*)

Little Robin Redbreast

Little Robin Redbreast
(*Make fist and join thumb and index fingers.*)
Sitting on a rail.
(*Rest wrist on edge of other hand.*)
Nibble, nabble goes his head.
(*Move thumb and index fingers up and down.*)
Wiggle, waggle goes his tail.
(*Tilt wrist over other hand.*)

This Little Calf

This little calf eats grass,
  (Extend fingers; push each down in turn.)
This little calf eats hay,
This little calf drinks water,
This little calf runs away,
This little calf does nothing
But just lies down all day.
  (Rest last finger in palm of other hand.)

The Family

Good Little Mother

Good little mother, how do you do?
    (Hold up one hand; wiggle each finger in turn.)
Dear strong daddy, glad to see you;
Big, tall brother, pleased you are here;
Kind little sister, you need not fear;
Glad welcome we'll give you, and baby dear too,
Yes, baby dear, how do you do?

40

Grandma's Spectacles

Here are Grandma's spectacles
(Make circles with thumbs and index fingers placed over eyes.)

And here is Grandma's hat;
(Join hands at finger tips and place on top of head.)

And here's the way she folds her hands
(Fold hands and place gently in lap.)

And puts them in her lap.

Here are Grandpa's spectacles,
(Make larger circles with thumbs and index fingers and place over eyes.)

And here is Grandpa's hat;
(Make larger pointed hat, as above.)

And here's the way he folds his arms
(Fold arms with vigor.)

And sits like that.

This Is the Mother

This is the mother, kind and dear,
(Make a fist, then point to thumb.)

This is the father, sitting near,
(Show each finger in turn.)

This is the brother, strong and tall,
This is the sister who plays with her ball,
This is the baby, the littlest of all,
See my whole family, large and small.
(Wiggle all the fingers.)

The Family

This is my father,
(Point to thumb.)

This is my mother,
(Point to index finger.)

This is my brother tall;
(Point to middle finger.)

This is my sister,
(Point to ring finger.)

This is the baby,
(Point to little finger.)

Oh! How we love them all.
(Clasp hands.)

Kitty, Kitty

Kitty, kitty, kitty, kitty,
(Extend one hand, palm up, fingers loosely curled.)
All my little ones so pretty;
You, and you, and you, and you,
(Point to children.)
Let me hear how you can mew.
Mew, mew, mew, mew.
(Children mew.)

Kitty, kitty, kitty, kitty,
All my little ones so pretty.

Curl up close now, just like that,
(Curl fingers around thumb.)
"Go to sleep," says mother cat,
(Close eyes.)
"Sleep till someone calls out, Scat!"
(Open eyes and hand suddenly.)

Chickens

One, two, three little chickens,
(Count three fingers.)
Dear little downy things,
Cuddling away from every danger
(Nestle one hand under other arm.)
Under their mother's wings.
Peep, peep, when the baby's sleepy,
This is the song he sings.
(Assume attitude of relaxation.)
Sleep, sleep, sleep, little chicks,
Little chicks sleep in the night.

Sleepy Fingers

My fingers are so sleepy
(Hold hand palm up, fingers loosely bent.)
It's time they went to bed.
So first you, Baby Finger,
(Put each finger down in palm of hand as rhyme indicates.)
Tuck in your little head.

Ring Man, now it's your turn,
And then come, Tall Man great;
Now, Pointer Finger, hurry
Because it's getting late.

Let's see if all are snuggled,
No, here's one more to come,
So come, lie close, little brother,
Make room for Master Thumb.

Bunnies' Bedtime

"My bunnies now must go to bed,"
(Hold up hand; extend fingers.)
The little mother rabbit said.
"But I will count them first to see
(Point to fingers.)
If they have all come back to me.
One bunny, two bunnies, three bunnies dear,
(Point to each finger as you count.)
Four bunnies, five bunnies—yes, all are here.
They are the prettiest things alive—
My bunnies, one, two, three, four, five."
(Point to each finger again.)

(When counting out, point to each child.)

Rock-a-Bye Baby, Thy Cradle Is Green

Rock-a-bye baby, thy cradle is green,
(Fold arms and rock them.)

Father's a nobleman, mother's a queen;

And Betty's a lady and wears a gold ring,
*(Make ring with thumb and index finger on one
hand; slide it over ring finger of other hand.)*

And Johnnie's a drummer and drums for the king.
(Beat hands as though beating a drum.)

44

The
World Outdoors

My Garden

This is my garden;
>   *(Extend one hand forward, palm up.)*

I'll rake it with care,
>   *(Make raking motion on palm with
>   three fingers of other hand.)*

And then some flower seeds
>   *(Make "planting" motion with thumb
>   and index finger of same hand.)*

I'll plant in there.
The sun will shine
>   *(Make circle above head with hands.)*

And the rain will fall,
>   *(Let fingers flutter down to lap.)*

And my garden will blossom
>   *(Cup hands together; extend upward slowly.)*

And grow straight and tall.

Pitter-Pat

Pitter-pat, pitter-pat, oh so many hours,
>   *(Let fingers patter on floor, table, hand, etc.)*

Although it keeps me in the house,
It's very good for flowers.
>   *(Cup hands and extend slowly upward.)*

Raindrops

Rain is falling down, rain is falling down.
> *(Raise arms, flutter fingers to ground
> tapping floor, or tap palm of hand.)*

Pitter-patter, pitter-patter,
Rain is falling down.

Whirling Leaves

The little leaves are whirling round, round, round,
> *(Flutter fingers above head and to ground.)*

The little leaves are whirling round, falling to the ground.
Round, round, round, round,
Falling to the ground.
> *(Whisper.)*

October

The month is October
> *(Flutter fingers.)*

With leaves falling down
That once were all
Yellow and scarlet and brown.

Leaves

The leaves are dropping from the trees,
> *(Flutter fingers up in air and to ground.)*

Yellow, brown, and red.
They patter softly like the rain;
> *(Tap fingers on floor.)*

One landed on my head.
> *(Tap head.)*

Falling Leaves

Many leaves are falling down,
> *(Flutter fingers from above head down
> to floor several times.)*

Yellow, red and even brown.
Falling on the frosty ground.
Falling on the frosty ground.

47

Snowflakes

Snowflakes whirling all around, all around, all around,
> *(Flutter fingers high above head, in the air,
> slowly falling to ground.)*

Snowflakes whirling all around
Until they cover all the ground.

Snow Men

Five little snow men
> *(Hold up one hand, fingers extended.)*

Standing in a row,
Each with a hat
> *(Join thumbs and index fingers and place on top of head.)*

And a big red bow.
> *(Join thumbs and index fingers together to make
> bow under chin.)*

Five little snow men
> *(Hold up one hand, fingers extended.)*

Dressed for a show,
Now they are ready,
Where will they go?
Wait till the sun shines;
> *(Make circle with arms above head.)*

Soon they will go
Down through the fields
> *(Bring arms down to lap.)*

With the melting snow.

Apples

Way up high in the apple tree
> *(Raise arms high above head, index fingers
> and thumbs making a circle.)*

Two little apples smiled at me.
I shook that tree as hard as I could,
> *(Shake arms.)*

And down came the apples;
> *(Drop one arm to knee; then drop other.)*

M . . . m . . . m . . . were they good!

Big People,
Little People

People

Big people, little people,
> *(Hold thumb and index fingers apart horizontally, then close together.)*

Fat people, skinny.
> *(Hold index fingers apart vertically; then close together.)*

Grumpy people, happy people,
> *(Make appropriate facial expressions.)*

People who are grinny.
Rushy people, slow people,
> *(Walk fingers of one hand up and down other arm as rhyme indicates.)*

Walking up and down.
Babies in their carriages
> *(Move one fist slowly up and down other arm.)*

Being pushed through town.

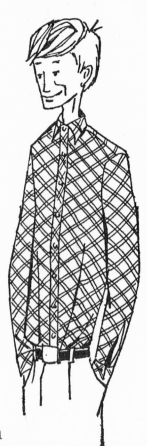

The Stilt Man

There was a great big stilt man
> *(Hold loose fists forward with index fingers extended one a bit above the other.)*

Who was tall, t-a-l-l, t-a-l-l,
> *(Widen distance between fingers.)*

There was a little midget
> *(Bring fingers close together.)*

Who was small, small, small.
And the midget who was small
> *(Wiggle bottom finger.)*

Would try and t-r-y, and t-r-y,
> *(Move bottom finger up a bit.)*

To reach up to the stilt man
> *(Keep moving top finger farther away.)*

Who was tall, t-a-l-l, t-a-l-l.

Aiken Drum

There was a man lived in the moon,
(Form circle over head with arms.)
And his name was Aiken Drum.
And he played upon a ladle,
(Pretend to strum musical instrument.)
And his name was Aiken Drum.
And his hat was made of good green cheese,
(Rest hands on head.)
And his name was Aiken Drum.
And his coat was made of good roast beef,
(Point to coat.)
And his name was Aiken Drum.
And his buttons were made of penny loaves,
(Point to buttons.)
And his name was Aiken Drum.
And his waistcoat was made of crusts of pie,
(Point to waistcoat.)
And his name was Aiken Drum.
And his britches were made of haggis bags,
(Point to pants.)
And his name was Aiken Drum.
There was a man lived in the moon,
(Form circle over head with arms; then drop them into lap.)
And his name was Aiken Drum.

Jack and Jill

Jack and Jill went up the hill
(Extend hands out flat, palms facing down;
climb them upwards.)

To fetch a pail of water,
Jack fell down and broke his crown,
(Let one hand fall quickly into lap.)

And Jill came tumbling after.
(Let other hand follow jerkily.)

Up Jack got and said to Jill
(Raise one hand and then the other.)

As in his arms he caught her,
(Cross arms and hug shoulders.)

"If you're not hurt, brush off the dirt,
(Brush off clothes.)

And then we'll fetch the water."

S-l-o-w-l-y, s-l-o-w-l-y, up the hill,
(Climb hands up slowly.)

This time they spilled no water.
They took it home to mother dear,
(Close fist and seem to carry bucket.)

Who kissed her son and daughter.
(Kissing sound.)

Rock-a-Bye Baby

Rock-a-bye baby,
(Fold arms and rock.)

On the treetop.
When the wind blows
The cradle will rock.
When the bough bends
(Bend forward.)

The cradle will fall,
(Open arms.)

And down will come baby,
(Drop arms to lap.)

Cradle and all.

Here Is the Church

Here is the church,
(Put backs of hands together, palms down.)

Here is the steeple.
(Clasp fingers; extend index fingers to make a point.)

Open the door,
(Turn hands around, fingers still clasped.)

And see all the people.
(Wiggle fingers.)

Ten Little Firemen

Ten little firemen
Sleeping in a row;
*(Extend both hands, fingers curled,
to represent sleeping men.)*

Ding, dong goes the bell,
(Pull bell cord with one hand.)

And down the pole they go.
*(Close both fists, put one on top of other,
slide them down pole.)*

Off on the engine, oh, oh, oh,
(Steer engine with hands.)

Using the big hose, so, so, so.
(Make nozzle with fist.)

When all the fire's out, home so-o slow.
(Steer engine with hands.)

Back to bed, all in a row.
(Extend both hands, fingers curled.)

King of France

The famous King of France,
He led ten thousand men.
He marched them way, way up the hill
(March hands up in air, one over other.)

And marched them down again.
(March hands down.)

And when they were up they were up, up, up;
(March hands up.)

And when they were down they were down,
  down, down;
(March hands down.)

And when they were only halfway up,
(Hold hand halfway up.)

They were neither up nor down.
(Move hand up, then down, very quickly.)

Playmates

A little boy lived in this house.
(Make fist with right hand, thumb hidden.)

A little girl lived in this house.
(Make fist with left hand, thumb hidden.)

The little boy came out of his house.
(Release right thumb.)

He looked up and down the street.
(Move thumb slowly.)

He didn't see any one, so he went back into his house.
(Tuck thumb back into fist.)

The little girl came out of her house.
(Release left thumb.)

She looked up and down the street.
(Move thumb slowly.)

She didn't see anyone, so she went back into her house.
(Tuck thumb back into fist.)

The next day the little boy came out of his house and looked **all around**.
(Release right thumb and move slowly.)

The little girl came out of her house and looked **all around**.
(Release left thumb and move slowly.)

They saw each other.
(Point thumbs toward each other.)

They walked across the street and shook hands.
(Move thumbs toward each other until they meet.)

Then the little boy went back into his house.
(Tuck right thumb back into fist.)

The little girl went back into her house.
(Tuck left thumb back into fist.)

54

Sing a Song of Sixpence

Sing a song of sixpence, a pocket full of rye,
(Make circle with hands.)

Four and twenty blackbirds baked in a pie.

When the pie was opened,
(Open hands.)

The birds began to sing.
(Flutter fingers.)

Wasn't that a dainty dish to set before a king?

The king was in his counting house,
(Cup one hand loosely.)

Counting out his money.
(Pick up "money" with other.)

The queen was in the parlor,

Eating bread and honey.
(Make eating motions.)

The maid was in the garden,

Hanging out the clothes,
(Hands extended up.)

When down came a blackbird,
(Flutter one hand down.)

And nipped off her nose!
(Nip nose.)

Warm Hands

Warm hands, warm—
(Put hands together.)

Do you know how?

If you want to

Warm your hands,

Warm your hands now.

Jack-in-the-Box

Jack-in-the-box, all shut up tight,
*(Close fist with thumb tucked in;
cover with flat palm of other hand.)*

Not a breath of air or a ray of light,

How tired he must be, all folded up.

Let's open the lid,
(Raise hand slightly.)

And up he'll jump.
(Remove hand quickly and pop up other thumb.)

Jonathan Bing

Poor old Jonathan Bing,
Went out in his carriage to visit the king.
But everyone pointed and said, "Look at that.
  (Point.)
Jonathan Bing has forgotten his hat."
  (Join thumb and index fingers and place on top of head.)
Poor old Jonathan Bing,
Went home and put on a new hat for the king.
  (Join thumb and index fingers and place on top of head.)
But when he arrived an archbishop said, "Hi,
Jonathan Bing, you've forgotten your tie."
  (Point to neck.)
Poor old Jonathan Bing,
Went home and put on a tie for the king.
  (Point to neck.)
But when he arrived a soldier said, "Ho,
You can't see the king in pajamas, you know."
  (Draw hands down body and legs.)
Poor old Jonathan Bing,
Went home and addressed a short note to the king.
  (Wiggle index finger along palm of other hand.)
"If you please will excuse me, I won't come to tea,
For home is the best place for people like *me*!"
  (Point to self.)

56

Snip, Snip, Snip, Snippety

Snip, snip, snip, snippety,
> *(Make a fist; extend index and tall fingers horizontally, and move back and forth for scissors.)*

Snip, snip, snip, snippety,
Here is dear Nancy,* all shaven and shorn.
> *(Move fingers lightly over other fist.)*

Creeping Indians

The Indians are creeping,
> *(Creep fingers along forearm.)*

Shh. . . . Shh. . . . shh. . . .
> *(Raise fingers to lips.)*

The Indians are creeping,
> *(Repeat first instruction.)*

Shh. . . . Shh. . . . shh. . . . shh. .
> *(Repeat second instruction.)*

They do not make a sound
As their feet touch the ground.
The Indians are creeping,
> *(Repeat first instruction.)*

Shh. . . . Shh. . . . shh.
> *(Repeat second instruction.)*

Thieken Man

Thieken man, build the barn,
> *(Hammer one fist on other.)*

Thuin man, spool the yarn,
> *(Make winding motion with hands.)*

Longen man, stir the brew,
> *(Make stirring motion with hands.)*

Gouten man, make a shoe,
> *(Tap shoe sole.)*

Little man, all for you.
> *(Point to child.)*

Said This Little Fairy

Said this little fairy, "I'm as thirsty as can be."
> *(Point to each finger.)*

Said this little fairy, "I'm hungry, too, dear me!"
Said this little fairy, "Who'll tell us where to go?"
Said this little fairy, "I'm sure that I don't know."
Said this little fairy, "Let's brew some dewdrop tea."
So they sipped it and ate honey beneath the maple tree.
> *(Make drinking and eating motions.)*

* *Substitute child's name.*

Shiver and Quiver

When it's cold, you shiver and you quiver.
  B-r-r-r, b-r-r-r, b-r-r-r.
    (Clasp arms and shiver.)
When it's cold, you shiver and you quiver.
  B-r-r-r, b-r-r-r, b-r-r-r
Your hands feel just like ice
    (Rub hands vigorously.)
So you rub them once or twice.
When it's cold, you shiver and you quiver.
  B-r-r-r, b-r-r-r, b-r-r-r!

Counting
and
Counting
Out

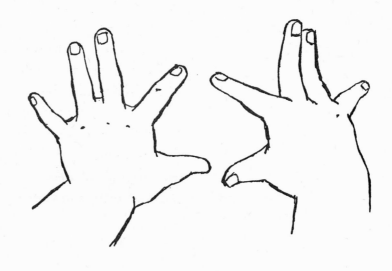

Catching a Fish

One, two, three, four, five,
(Count out fingers on right hand.)
I caught a little fish alive.
(Catch all fingers on right hand with left hand.)
Why did you let it go?
(Release fingers suddenly.)
Because it bit my finger so.
(Shake right hand.)
Which finger did it bite?
The little finger on the right.
(Point to little finger on right hand.)

Chickadees

Five little chickadees sitting on the floor;
(Hold up hand, fingers extended.)
One flew away and then there were four.
(Fold down one finger as each bird flies away.)
Four little chickadees sitting in a tree;
One flew away and then there were three.
Three little chickadees looking at you;
One flew away and then there were two.
Two little chickadees sitting in the sun;
One flew away and then there was one.
One little chickadee sitting all alone;
He flew away and then there was none.

Five Little Indians

Five little Indians running through a door,
(Hold up one hand, fingers extended.)

One fell down and then there were four.
(Tuck one finger in palm, for each line,
until all make a fist.)

Four little Indians in an apple tree,

One fell out and then there were three.

Three little Indians stirring up some stew,

One fell in and then there were two.

Two little Indians playing with a gun,

One pulled the trigger and then there was one.

One little Indian left all alone,

He went home and then there was none.

Frogs

One, two, three, four, five.
(Count fingers.)
Five little frogs standing in a row.
This little frog stubbed his toe;
(Point to each finger in turn.)
This little frog said, "Oh, oh, oh";
This little frog laughed and was glad;
This little frog cried and was sad;
This little frog, so thoughtful and good,
Ran for the doctor as fast as he could.

Five Little Froggies

Five little froggies sat on the shore,
*(Open hand; extend fingers. Push down one finger
as each frog leaves.)*
One went for a swim and then there were four.
Four little froggies looked out to sea,
One went swimming, and then there were three.
Three little froggies said, "What can we do?"
One jumped in the water and then there were two.
Two little froggies sat in the sun,
One swam off and then there was one.
One lonely froggie said, "This is no fun."
He dived into the water and then there was none.

B.D.

Five Little Squirrels

One, two, three, four, five,
> *(Count fingers; then point to each in turn.)*

Five little squirrels sitting in a tree;
Said this little squirrel, "What do I see?"
Said this little squirrel, "I see a gun."
Said this little squirrel, "Oh! Let's run."
Said this little squirrel, "I'm not afraid."
Said this little squirrel, "Let's sit in the shade."
Bang! Went the gun and they all ran away.
> *(Clap hands slowly and hide behind back.)*

Five Little Ants

Five little ants in an ant hill,
> *(Close fist, palm down.)*

Busily working and never still.
> *(Wiggle knuckles.)*

Do you think they are alive?
See them come out—
One, two, three, four, five.
> *(Bring fingers out one at a time.)*

These five little ants near an ant hill,
> *(Wiggle fingers of one hand toward closed fist of other.)*

Run as hard and run with a will
To gather food to keep alive.
Now they go in—
> *(Close fingers in fist again.)*

One, two, three, four, five.

I Caught a Hare

One, two, three, four, five;
(Count fingers on one hand.)

I caught a hare alive.
(Close fist.)

Six, seven, eight, nine, ten;
(Count fingers on other hand.)

I let it go again.
(Hold up ten fingers.)

Five Little Kittens

Five little kittens standing in a row,
(Extend left fingers upward, palm out.)

They nod their heads to the children, so.
(Bend fingers forward.)

They run to the left, they run to the right,
(Wiggle fingers to left; then to right.)

They stand up and stretch in the bright sunlight.
(Stretch fingers slowly.)

Along comes a dog, who's in for some fun,
(Move right fist slowly toward stretching fingers.)

M-e-o-w, see those kittens run.
(Run left fingers behind back.)

Great Big Ball

A great big ball,
(Join hands, finger tips touching to make a big ball.)

A middle-sized ball,
(Make smaller ball.)

A little ball I see.
(Join thumb and index finger of one hand to make little ball.)

Let's see if we can count them;
(Make each of the three balls as they are counted.)

One, two, three.

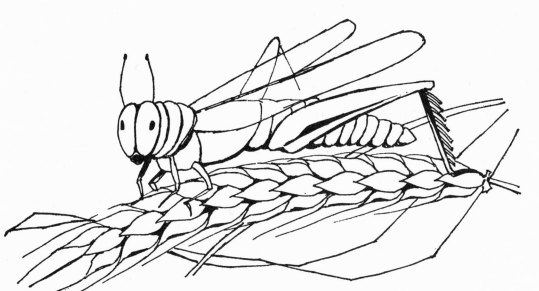

Grasshoppers

Ten little grasshoppers sitting on a vine;
(Hold up ten fingers; fold one down at each count.)
One ate too much corn, and then there were nine.
Nine little grasshoppers swinging on a gate;
One fell off, then there were eight.
Eight little grasshoppers started off to Devon;
One lost his way, then there were seven.
Seven little grasshoppers lived between two bricks;
Along came a windstorm, then there were six.
Six little grasshoppers found a beehive;
One found a bumblebee, then there were five.
Five little grasshoppers playing on the floor;
Pussycat passed that way, then there were four.
Four little grasshoppers playing near a tree;
One chased a buzzy fly, then there were three.
Three little grasshoppers looked for pastures new;
A turkey gobbler saw them, then there were two.
Two little grasshoppers sitting in the sun;
A little boy went fishing, then there was one.
One little grasshopper left all alone;
He tried to find his brothers, then there was none.

One, Two, Buckle My Shoe

One, two, buckle my shoe,
  (Follow action as rhyme indicates.)
Three, four, knock at the door,
Five, six, pick up sticks,
Seven, eight, lay them straight,
Nine, ten, a big fat hen.
  (Extend hands, finger tips touching.)

Telegraph Poles

Here are two telegraph poles,
  (Raise index fingers.)
Between them a wire strung,
  (Put middle fingers together, index fingers raised.)
Two little birds hopped right on
  (Place thumbs on middle fingers.)
And swung, and swung, and swung.
  (Swing hands back and forth.)

Hot Cross Buns

Hot cross buns,
  (Clap hands in rhythm.)
Hot cross buns,
One a-penny, two a-penny,
  (Count out two fingers.)
Hot cross buns.
  (Clap hands.)

Soldiers

Five little soldiers standing in a row,
  (Hold up fingers of one hand.)
Three stood straight
  (Hold three fingers straight.)
And two stood so.
  (Bend two fingers.)
Along came the captain
  (Extend index finger on other hand and move in front of first hand.)
And what do you think?
They all stood straight, as quick as a wink.
  (Hold all five fingers up straight.)

Johnny's Hammer

Johnny works with one hammer, one hammer, one hammer,
(Hammer fist with thumb of other hand.)
Johnny works with one hammer, this fine day.

Johnny works with two hammers, two hammers, two hammers,
(Hammer fist with thumb and index finger of other hand.)
Johnny works with two hammers, this fine day.

Johnny works with three hammers, three hammers, three hammers,
(Add one finger each time until all fingers are hammering.)
Johnny works with three hammers, this fine day.

Johnny works with four hammers, four hammers, four hammers,
Johnny works with four hammers, this fine day.

Johnny works with five hammers, five hammers, five hammers,
Johnny works with five hammers, this fine day.

Johnny now is so tired, so tired, so tired,
(Hold hammering position.)
Johnny now is so tired, this fine day.

Johnny goes to sleep now, sleep now, sleep now,
(Nod head and close eyes.)
Johnny goes to sleep now, this fine day.

Johnny's waking up now, up now, up now,
(Wake up smiling.)
Johnny's waking up now, this fine day.

This Old Man

This old man, he played one,
(Hold up one finger.)

He played knick-knack on his thumb.
(Tap thumbs together.)

Knick-knack, paddy-whack, give a dog a bone,
(Tap knees, clap hands, extend one hand.)

This old man came rolling home.
(Roll hands.)

This old man, he played two,
(Hold up two fingers.)

He played knick-knack on his shoe.
(Tap shoe.)
(Repeat lines 3 and 4 above.)

This old man, he played three,
(Hold up three fingers.)

He played knick-knack on his knee.
(Tap knee.)
(Repeat lines 3 and 4 above.)

This old man, he played four,
(Hold up four fingers.)

He played knick-knack on the floor.
(Tap floor.)
(Repeat lines 3 and 4 above.)

This old man, he played five,
(Hold up five fingers.)

He played knick-knack on his drive
(Tap floor.)
(Repeat lines 3 and 4 above.)

This old man, he played six,
(Hold up six fingers.)

He played knick-knack on his sticks.
(Tap index fingers.)
(Repeat lines 3 and 4 above.)

This old man, he played seven,
  (Hold up seven fingers.)

He played knick-knack along to Devon.
  (Point outward.)
  (Repeat lines 3 and 4 above.)

This old man, he played eight,
  (Hold up eight fingers.)

He played knick-knack on his pate.
  (Tap head.)
  (Repeat lines 3 and 4 above.)

This old man, he played nine,
  (Hold up nine fingers.)

He played knick-knack on his spine.
  (Tap spine.)
  (Repeat lines 3 and 4 above.)

This old man, he played ten,
  (Hold up ten fingers.)

He played knick-knack now and then.
  (Clap hands.)
  (Repeat lines 3 and 4.)

Ten Little Indians

One little, two little, three little Indians;
  (Show a finger at each count.)
Four little, five little, six little Indians;
Seven little, eight little, nine little Indians;
Ten little Indian boys.

Ten Little Men

Ten little Men standing in a row,
   (Hold up ten fingers.)
Ten little Men to market go,
   (Move hands sideways, and return.)
Thumbkin goes to buy some meat,
   (Move each pair of fingers as rhyme indicates.)
Pointer goes to buy some wheat.
Tall Man goes to get a sack
In which to bring the bundles back.
Ring Man goes to get some peas.
Little Man goes to get some cheese.
Ten little Men standing in a row.
   (Hold up ten fingers.)
Ten little Men to market go.
   (Move fingers away behind back.)

One for the Money

One for the money,
   (Point to each finger.)
Two for the show,
Three to get ready,
And four to go.

Tennessee

One, I see,
   *(Close fists; extend each
   finger upward in
   turn as rhyme indicates.)*
Two, I see,
Three, I see,
Four, I see,
Five, I see,
Six, I see,
Seven, I see,
Eight, I see,
Nine, I see,
Tennessee!

Two Little Houses

Two little houses closed up tight,
   (Close fists over thumbs.)
Open up the windows and let in the light.
   (Open fists, hold fingers up, palms to front.)
Ten little finger people standing tall and straight,
   (Nod fingers and then straighten.)
Ready for school at half-past eight.
   (Move hands and arms jerkily forward.)

70

Counting Out

One, two, three, four, five, six, seven,
> (*Clap in rhythm; or if counting out,
> point to each child.*)

All good children go to Devon.
When they get there they will shout
O-U-T spells "out."

Two Little Ducks

Two little ducks that I once knew,
> (*Extend index and tall fingers; emphasize each duck.*)

Fat ducks, skinny ducks, there were two,
But the one little duck with the feathers on his back,
> (*Emphasize* ONE *with index finger.*)

He led the others with a quack, quack, quack.
> (*Bend arms at elbows, tuck hands in armpits,
> flap arms up and down.*)

Down to the river they would go,
> (*Put hands together and wiggle in front of body.*)

Wobble, wobble, wobble, wobble, to and fro,
But the one little duck with the feathers on his back,
> (*Emphasize* ONE.)

He led the others with a quack, quack, quack,
> (*Bend arms at elbows, tuck hands in armpits,
> flap arms up and down.*)

He led the others with a quack, quack, quack.

Two Mother Pigs

Two mother pigs lived in a pen,
(Show thumbs.)

Each had four babies, and that made ten.
(Show fingers and thumbs.)

These four babies were black as night,
(Hold one hand up, thumb in palm.)

These four babies were black and white.
(Hold other hand up, thumb in palm.)

But all eight babies loved to play

And they rolled and rolled in the mud all day.
(Roll hands over each other.)

At night, with their mother, they curled up in a heap,
(Make fists, palms up.)

And squealed and squealed till they went to sleep.

72

Bumblebee

Bee, bee, bumblebee.
(Make bee by resting index finger on thumb.)

Sting a man upon his knee.
("Sting" knee.)

Sting a pig upon his snout,
("Sting" nose.)

One, two, three, four, five—you're out!
(Point out each finger.)

(When counting out, point to each child.)

Eeny, Meeny, Miney, Mo

Eeny, meeny, miney, mo;
(Point out each finger.)

Catch a tiger by the toe;
("Catch" one finger as rhyme indicates.)

When he hollers let him go.
(Let go of finger.)

Eeny, meeny, miney, mo.
(Point out each finger.)
(For counting out, point to each child in turn.
Vary pointing by tapping shoes, etc.)

Two Little Blackbirds

Two little blackbirds sitting on a hill
(Close fists; extend thumbs.)

One named Jack and the other named Jill.
(Talk to each thumb.)

Fly away Jack; fly away Jill;
(Toss thumbs over shoulders separately.)

Come back Jack; come back Jill.
(Bring back fists separately with thumbs extended.)

73

Mary at the Cottage Door

One, two, three, four,
  (Count fingers.)
Mary at the cottage door,
Five, six, seven, eight,
Eating cherries off her plate.
  (Make eating motion with hand.)
  (For counting out, point to each child.)

Tee-Taw-Buck

One silk, two silk, three silk, zan,
  (Hold up one hand; point to each finger in turn.)
Four silk, five silk, tittum tan,
Harum, scarum, buckum, barum,
Tee-taw-buck.
  (Clap hands.)
  (When counting out, point to each child in turn.)

Ten Little Fishes

Ten little fishes were swimming in a school,
  (Point to each finger in turn.)
This one said, "Let's swim where it is cool."
This one said, "It's a very warm day."
This one said, "Come on, let's play."
This one said, "I'm as hungry as can be."
This one said, "There's a worm for me."
This one said, "Wait, we'd better look."
This one said, "Yes, it's on a hook."
This one said, "Can't we get it anyway?"
This one said, "Perhaps we may."
This one, so very brave, grabbed a bite and swam away.

Around the
House

The House

This is the roof of the house so good.
>*(Hold up hands, finger tips touching, hands spread apart at bottom.)*

These are the walls that are made of wood.
>*(Extend hands parallel.)*

These are the windows that let in the light.
>*(Make a square by extending index fingers up, thumbs out.)*

This is the door that shuts so tight.
>*(Make a square by extending index fingers up, thumbs out.)*

This is the chimney so straight and tall.
>*(Raise index finger.)*

What a good house for us, one and all!
>*(Extend hands in front, parallel to each other.)*

Up, Up

Here we go up, up, up.
>*(Follow action with hands as rhyme indicates.)*

Here we go down, down, down,
Here we go backward and forward,
And around and around.

Who Feels Happy?

Who feels happy, who feels gay?
All who do, clap their hands this way.
>*(Follow action as rhyme indicates.)*

Who feels happy, who feels gay?
All who do, nod their heads this way.

Who feels happy, who feels gay?
All who do, tap their shoulders this way.
>*(Children like to suggest things to do.)*

Swinging

Hold on tightly as we go,
     (Clasp hands in front and make a swing.)
Swinging high and swinging low.
     (Swing as rhyme indicates.)

The Seesaw

The seesaw goes up.
> *(Extend one arm up and one arm down.)*

The seesaw goes down.
> *(Reverse arm positions and continue action as rhyme indicates.)*

Seesaw up, and seesaw down,
Seesaw stops up,
One end on the ground!

The Window

See the window I have here,
> *(Make a window with thumbs touching and index fingers extended upward, and hold close to face.)*

So big and high and square;
I can stand in front of it,
And see the things out there.

Wind the Bobbin

Wind, wind, wind the bobbin,
> *(Spread apart thumb and index finger on one hand to hold "bobbin.")*

Wind, wind, wind the bobbin,
> *(Make rotating motion with other hand.)*

Pull, pull, and tap, tap, tap.
> *(Make fists and pull apart hard; then tap fists together.)*

Up the Steps We Go

Up the steps we will go,
> *(Climb palms of hands upwards.)*

Sometimes fast and sometimes slow,
Until we reach the top.
S-l-i-d-e down!
> *(Slide one palm down other arm.)*

Open, Close Them

Open, close them; open, close them;
> *(Hold palms up, fingers extended; then follow action as rhyme indicates.)*

Let your hands go "clap."
Open, close them; open, close them;
Drop them in your lap.
Walk them, walk them, walk them, walk them,
Way up to your chin.
Open up your little mouth,
But don't let them walk in.
Open, close them; open, close them;
To your shoulders fly.
Let them like the little birdies
Fly up to the sky.
Falling, falling, falling, falling,
Almost to the ground,
Quickly raising all your fingers,
Twirl them round and round.

Up a Step

Up a step, and up a step, and up a step, and up,
> *(Climb palms of hands upward.)*

I climb the ladder to the very tiptop.
Then I sit down and zi-p to the ground!
> *(Let one hand sit on other shoulder and slide down arm.)*

Pat-a-Cake

Pat-a-cake, pat-a-cake, baker's man,
    (Clap hands.)

Bake me a cake as fast as you can,
    (Cup one hand loosely, palm up; rotate finger of
    other hand in cupped palm.)

Pat it and prick it and mark it with "B"
    (Pat hands firmly.)

And put it in the oven for baby and me.
    (Move hand forward slowly.)

Good Morning

Good morning, good morning, good morning, now we'll say,
Good morning, good morning, we'll nod our heads this way.
    (Follow action as rhyme indicates.)

Good morning, good morning, good morning, now we'll say,
Good morning, good morning, we'll wave our hands this way.
Good morning, good morning, good morning, now we'll say,
Good morning, good morning, we'll throw a kiss this way.
    (Children love to name the activity.)

80

I Shut the Door

I shut the door and locked it tight,
> *(Make fist with one hand; insert other index finger
> in fist and turn.)*

And put the key out of sight.
> *(Withdraw index finger and hide behind back.)*

I found the key to open the door,
> *(Hold index finger in front.)*

And turned, and turned—and turned some more,
> *(Insert index finger in fist again, and turn.)*

And then I opened the door.

The Very Nicest Place

The fish lives in the brook,
> *(Put palms together tightly; wiggle forward.)*

The bird lives in the tree,
> *(Bend forearms at elbows and extend upwards;
> cup hands and spread open.)*

But home's the very nicest place
For a little child like me.
> *(Point to self.)*

Tap at the Door

Tap at the door,
> *(Tap one hand with fingers of other.)*

Peep in,
> *(Form fingers into rings around eyes.)*

Turn the knob,
> *(Make turning motion with other hand.)*

Walk in,
> *(Walk fingers of one hand on palm of other.)*

And—shut the door!
> *(Clap loudly.)*

Helpfulness

This little girl does nothing but play,
> *(Hold fingers of one hand up straight.*
> *Point to each finger in turn.)*

This little child wants her way,
This is a girl so strong and tall,
This child will not help at all.
Here's one who's kind and true,
Always helping, just like you.
> *(Point to child.)*

The Teapot

I'm a little teapot, short and stout.
This is my handle,
> *(Put one hand on hip.)*

This is my spout.
> *(Extend opposite arm sideways, hand out.)*

When I get all steamed up, then I shout.
Jut tip me over and pour me out.
> *(Bend body toward extended arm.)*

I'm a very clever pot, it is true.
Here's an example of what I can do.
I can change my handle and change my spout.
> *(Change position of hands.)*

Just tip me over and pour me out.
> *(Bend body in opposite direction.)*

The Little Wash Bench

Here's a little wash bench,
(Extend hands parallel, thumbs down.)

Here's a little tub,
(Make circle with fingers.)

Here's a little scrubbing board,
(Make square, hold index fingers up straight, extend thumbs to meet.)

And here's the way to rub.
(Make rubbing motions with fists.)

Here's a little cake of soap,
(Make cake of soap with thumb and index finger.)

Here's a dipper new.
(Cup fingers, hold hand close to body.)

Here's a basket wide and deep,
(Make circle with arms.)

And here are clothespins too.
(Extend index and tall fingers.)

Here's the line away up high,
(Make fists; join thumbs; hold up.)

Here are the clothes all drying.
(Extend rest of fingers down.)

Here's the sun so warm and bright,
(Hold arms above head in circle.)

And now the wash is drying.
(Join thumbs; drop fingers.)

Here's a Cup

Here's a cup, and here's a cup,
(Make circle with thumb and index finger of one hand; extend arm, and repeat.)

And here's a pot of tea.
(Make fist with other hand and extend thumb for spout.)

Pour a cup, and pour a cup,
(Tip fist to pour.)

And have a drink with me.
(Make drinking motions.)

We Wash Our Shirt

This is the way we wash our shirt,
Wash our shirt, wash our shirt,
*(Hold fists close together against lap and scrub
up and down.)*

This is the way we hang up our shirt,
Hang up our shirt, hang up our shirt,
(Raise arms as if pinning clothes on line.)

This is the way we take down our shirt,
Take down our shirt, take down our shirt,
(Raise arms as if removing clothes from line.)

This is the way we iron our shirt,
Iron our shirt, iron our shirt,
(Make a fist for iron and glide over other arm.)

This is the way we mend our shirt,
Mend our shirt, mend our shirt,
*(Hold one hand in front and make sewing motions
on it with other hand.)*

This is the way we fold our shirt,
Fold our shirt, fold our shirt,
(Make appropriate folding motions.)

This is the way we put on our shirt,
Put on our shirt, put on our shirt,
(Make appropriate dressing motions.)

And wear it all the day.
(Point to own clothes.)

Noise
Makers

The Finger Band

The finger band is coming to town,
> *(Put hands behind back; bring them out slowly and rhythmically, shaking fingers.)*

Coming to town, coming to town,
The finger band is coming to town
So early in the morning.

Here is the way they wear their caps,
> *(Bring hands to a point over head.)*

Wear their caps, wear their caps,
Here is the way they wear their caps
So early in the morning.

Here is the way they play their drums,
> *(Pretend to beat drums or any other instrument.)*

Play their drums, play their drums,
Here is the way they play their drums
So early in the morning.

The finger band is going away,
> *(Use soft voices as hands retreat.)*

Going away, going away,
The finger band is going away
So early in the morning.

The finger band has gone away,
> *(Use very soft voices; hands are now behind backs.)*

Gone away, gone away,
The finger band has gone away
So early in the morning.

I Am a Fine Musician

I am a fine musician, I travel round the world.
(Clap hands.)

I can play my violin, my violin, my violin.
*(Extend one arm for violin; move other hand
back and forth across arm.)*

I can play my violin, fiddle-dee-dee-da.

I am a fine musician, I travel round the world.
(Clap hands.)

I can blow my trumpet, my trumpet, my trumpet.
(Hold fist to mouth and blow.)

I can blow my trumpet, toot-toot-toot-toot-toot.

I am a fine musician, I travel round the world.
(Clap hands.)

I can crash my cymbals, my cymbals, my cymbals.
(Brush palms of hands up and down against each other.)

I can crash my cymbals, crash-crash-crash-crash-bang.

I am a fine musician, I travel round the world.
(Clap hands.)

I can beat my big loud drum, big loud drum, big loud drum,
(Beat drum.)

I can beat my big loud drum, boom-boom-boom-boom-boom.

Hammering

Bang, bang, with your hammer,
(Make fist with one hand; extend thumb up.

Pound, pound, pound the nail,
(Pound thumb with other fist.)

Pound the nail down tight.
(Pound thumb slowly down into fist.)

Peas Porridge

Peas porridge hot,
(Clap hands in rhythm.)

Peas porridge cold,

Peas porridge in the pot
(Cup two hands to make pot.)

Nine days old.

Some like it hot,
*(Cup one hand; dip other index finger into
"bowl" and up to mouth as if eating.)*

Some like it cold,

Some like it in the pot
(Cup two hands again.)

Nine days old.

Shake, Shake, Knock, Knock

Shake, shake, knock, knock,
*(Raise one fist and shake; then knock fist
on open palm of other hand.)*

Shake, shake, knock, knock,

I play on my tambourine.

Shake, shake, knock, knock,

Shake, shake, knock, knock,

I play on my tambourine.

Ten Little Soldiers

Ten little soldiers standing in a row.
(Extend all fingers up, palms out.)

They all bow down to the captain—so.
(Bend fingers at knuckles.)

They march to the left, they march to the right.
(Straighten fingers and move to left and then to right.)

They all stand straight quite ready to fight.
(All fingers stand still.)

Along comes a man with a great big gun.

"Bang!" You ought to see those soldiers run.
(Clap at "bang.")

Pound Goes the Hammer

Pound pound pound pound pound goes the hammer,
(Hammer one fist with other.)

Pound pound pound pound pound pound pound.

Bzz bzz bzz bzz bzz goes the big saw,
*(Open hand and make sawing motion
across other arm.)*

Bzz bzz bzz bzz bzz bzz bzz.

Chop chop chop chop chop goes the big axe,
*(Put one fist on top of other as though holding
an axe and make chopping motion.)*

Chop chop chop chop chop chop chop.

Balloons

This is the way we blow our balloon; blow, blow, blow.
*(Hold hands to mouth, palms flat together, blow
into hands, separating them a bit while blowing.)*

This is the way we break our balloon; oh, oh, oh!
(Clap hands.)

Let Your Hands Clap

Let your hands clap, clap, clap,
(Clap hands three times.)

Let your fingers tap, tap, tap,
(Tap fingers three times.)

Fold your arms and quiet be.
(Fold arms.)

Roll your hands so wide awake,
(Roll hands.)

Let your fingers shake, shake, shake,
(Shake fingers.)

Climb the ladder, do not fall,
(Hold hands open, palms down; step one over other high above head.)

Till we reach the steeple tall.

Fold your hands and quiet be.
(Fold hands.)

Indians

Ten little Indians standing in a row;
(Hold up ten fingers.)

They all bow down to their chief, just so.
(Bend down ten fingers.)

They march to the left,
(Move both hands to the left with fingers held up.)

They march to the right,
(Move both hands to right with fingers held up.)

This is the way they learn to fight.
(Tap fingers together.)

Along comes a cowboy with a great big gun;
(Point index finger.)

Boom, boom, boom, and away they all run.
(Index finger shoots; then fingers on both hands run away.)

Holidays
and
Special
Occasions

Christmas Is A-Coming

Christmas is a-coming,
The geese are getting fat.
 (Cup hands, palms facing each other.)

Please to put a penny in the old man's hat.
 *(Hold one palm open; join thumb and index finger of
 other, and lay in open palm.)*

If you haven't got a penny,
 (Tap palm.)

A ha'penny will do.
 (Tap palm.)

If you haven't got a ha'penny,
 (Tap palm.)

God bless you.
 (Point to child.)

Christmas Bells

Hear the merry Christmas bells
 *(Pretend to hold bells in
 hands and shake them.)*

Ding, dong, ding, dong, ding, dong dell.
Ringing while the children sing,
Ring, ring, ring, ring, ring, ring, ring!

Santa Claus

Down the chimney dear Santa Claus crept,
 *(Make loose fist with left hand; insert right-
 hand finger into it.)*

Into the room where the children slept.
 (Place three fingers of right hand on palm of left.)

He saw their stockings hung in a line
 (Suspend three fingers of left hand.)

And he filled them with candies and goodies.
 (Make motions as if filling stockings.)

Altho' he counted them: one, two, three,
 (Indicate by counting fingers.)

The baby's stocking he could not see.
"Ho! Ho!" said Santa Claus, "That won't do."
So he popped her present right into her shoe.
 *(Cup left hand and put finger of right
 hand into it.)*

Christmas Tree

Here stands a lovely Christmas tree,
Christmas tree, Christmas tree,
    (Hold hands up, finger tips touching.)
Here stands a lovely Christmas tree,
So early in the morning.

Here is a horn for the Christmas tree,
Christmas tree, Christmas tree,
    (Hold fist to mouth and blow.)
Here is a horn for the Christmas tree,
So early in the morning.

Here is a drum for the Christmas Tree,
Christmas tree, Christmas tree,
    (Beat drum.)
Here is a drum for the Christmas tree,
So early in the morning.

Here are the lights for the Christmas tree,
Christmas tree, Christmas tree,
    (Flutter fingers.)
Here are the lights for the Christmas tree,
So early in the morning.

Here stands a lovely Christmas tree,
Christmas tree, Christmas tree,
    (Hold hands up, finger tips touching.)
Here stands a lovely Christmas tree
So early in the morning.

Here Is the Chimney

Here is the chimney,
> *(Make fist, enclosing thumb.)*

Here is the top,
> *(Place palm of other hand on top of fist.)*

Open the lid,
> *(Remove top hand quickly.)*

And out Santa will pop.
> *(Pop up thumb.)*

Little Jack Horner

Little Jack Horner
> *(Cup hand to make pie. Make eating motion
> with other hand.)*

Sat in a corner
Eating his Christmas pie.
He stuck in his thumb
> *(Insert thumb in other fist.)*

And pulled out a plum
> *(Pull thumb out of fist; make circle with same
> thumb and index finger, and hold it up.)*

And said, "What a good boy am I."

Our Table

Every day when we eat our dinner
Our table is very small.
> *(Show with hands.)*

There's room for father, mother, brother,
> *(Point to each finger.)*

Sister, and me—that's all.
But when Thanksgiving Day, and the company comes,
You'd scarcely believe your eyes;
For that very same table stretches
Until it is just this size.
> *(Show with hands spread wider.)*

I've a Jack-o'-Lantern

I've a jack-o'-lantern,
(Make ball with open fist, thumb at top.)
With a great, big grin.
(Grin.)
I've a jack-o'-lantern with a candle in.
(Insert other index finger up through bottom of fist.)

Halloween Witches

One little, two little, three little witches;
(Hold up one hand; nod fingers at each count.)
Fly over haystacks,
(Fly hand in up-and-down motion.)
Fly over ditches.
Slide down moonbeams without any hitches,
(Glide hand downward.)
Heigh-ho! Halloween's here.

Jack-o'-Lanterns

Five little jack-o'-lanterns sitting on a gate.
(Hold up five fingers.)
The first one said, "Oh my, it's getting late."
(Point to each finger in turn.)
The second one said, "Let's have some fun."
The third one said, "Let's run, let's run."
The fourth one said, "Let's dance, let's prance."
The fifth one said, "Now is our chance."
When "Who-o-o" went the wind,
(Blow hard.)
And out went the light,
And away went the jack-o'-lanterns on Halloween night.
(Run fingers behind back.)

Witch's Cat

I am the witch's cat.

(Make a fist with two fingers extended for cat.)

Miaow, miaow.

(Stroke fist with other hand.)

My fur is black as darkest night.

My eyes are glaring green and bright.

(Circle eyes with thumbs and forefingers.)

I am the witch's cat.

(Make a fist again with two fingers extended, and stroke fist with other hand.)

My Pumpkin

See my pumpkin round and fat.
> *(Make circle with hands, fingers spread wide, touching.)*

See my pumpkin yellow.
> *(Make smaller circle.)*

Watch him grin on Halloween.
> *(Point to mouth which is grinning wide.)*

He's a very funny fellow.

Very Nice Jack-o'-Lantern

This is a very nice jack-o'-lantern,
> *(Cup fingers of one hand to make jack-o'-lantern.)*

These are the eyes of the jack-o'-lantern,
> *(Outline eyes on cupped fingers.)*

This is the nose of the jack-o'-lantern,
> *(Outline nose.)*

This is the mouth of the jack-o'-lantern,
> *(Outline mouth.)*

And this is where the candle goes.
> *(Insert index finger in center of cupped hand for candle.)*

The Friendly Ghost

I'm a friendly ghost—almost!
> *(Point to self.)*

And I can chase you, too!
> *(Point to child.)*

I'll just cover me with a sheet
> *(Pretend to cover self, ending with hands covering face.)*

And then call "Scat" to you.
> *(Uncover face quickly and call out "Scat.")*

Scary Eyes

See my big and scary eyes.
> *(Circle thumb and index fingers around eyes.)*

Look out now

A big surprise——Boo!
> *(Pull hands away, shout "Boo!")*

Witch

If I were a witch,
> (*One fist rides on top of other, waving through air.*)

I'd ride on a broom
And scatter the ghosts
With a zoom, zoom, zoom.

Coal-Black Cat

Coal-black cat with humped-up back,
> (*Hold tight fist downward.*)

Shining eyes so yellow;
> (*Hold hands to eyes.*)

See him with his funny tail.
> (*Poke index finger of one hand through fist of other and wiggle end of finger.*)

He's a funny fellow.

98

Make a Valentine

Snip, snip, snip the paper.
> *(Extend index and middle fingers horizontally,
> and move up and down.)*

Paste, paste, paste the paper.
> *(Move index finger over palm of other hand.)*

Press, press, press the paper.
> *(Press palm of one hand into other.)*

Here's a valentine for you.

Valentine's Good Morning

Good morning to you, Valentine,
Curl your locks as I do mine;
> *(Point to curls.)*

Two before, and three behind.
> *(Point in front of shoulder and indicate "two,"
> then in back of shoulder and indicate "three.")*

Good morning to you, Valentine.

Valentine for You

A valentine for you,
> *(Let thumb and index finger touch
> to make square.)*

A valentine for you,
> *(Pass "valentine" to each child.)*

A valentine, a valentine,
A valentine for you.

The Circus

Going to the circus to have a lot of fun:
    (Hold up closed fists.)
The animals parading, one by one.
    (Raise fingers to indicate each new number.)
Now they're walking two by two,
A great big lion and a caribou.

Now they're walking three by three,
The elephants and the chimpanzee.

Now they walking four by four,
A stripy tiger and a big old boar.

Now they're walking five by five,
Makes us laugh when they arrive.

Now they're walking six by six,
Little dogs jump over sticks.

Now they're walking seven by seven,
Zebras stamping on to Devon.

Now they're walking eight by eight,
Running and jumping over the gate.

Now they're walking nine by nine,
Scary rabbit and the porcupine.

Now they're walking ten by ten,
Ready to start all over again.

Five Years Old

Please, everybody, look at me!
(Point to self.)

Today I'm five years old, you see!
(Hold up five fingers.)

And after this, I won't be four,
(Hold up four fingers.)

Not ever, ever, any more!

I won't be three—or two—or one,
(Hold up three, then two, then one.)

For that was when I'd first begun.

Now I'll be five a while, and then
(Hold up five fingers.)

I'll soon be something else again!

Bedtime

This little fellow is ready for bed,
(Extend index finger.)

Down on the pillow he lays his head;
(Lay finger in palm of other hand.)

Pulls up the covers, snug and tight,
(Close fingers over "fellow" in palm.)

And this is the way he sleeps all night.
(Close eyes.)

Morning comes and he opens his eyes,
(Open eyes.)

Quickly he pushes the covers aside;
(Open fingers.)

Jumps out of bed, puts on his clothes,
(Let opposite hand dress "fellow.")

And this is the way to school he goes.
(Walk two fingers up opposite arm.)

Index of First Lines

A great big ball, 64
A kitten is hiding under a chair, 32
A little boy lived in this house, 54
A little doggie all brown and black, 30
A valentine for you, 99
Auto, auto, may I have a ride?, 24

Bang, bang, with your hammer, 88
Bee, bee, bumblebee, 73
Big clocks make a sound, 27
Big people, little people, 50

Children put your pants on, 16
Choo, choo, choo, 22
Christmas is a-coming, 92
Clap your hands, clap your hands, 10
Coal-black cat with humped-up back, 98
Cobbler, cobbler, mend my shoe, 18
Come follow, follow, follow, 9

Down by the station, 22
Down the chimney dear Santa Claus crept, 92

Eensy, weensy spider, 31
Eeny, meeny, miney, mo, 73
Every day when we eat our dinner, 94
Eye Winker, 11

Fee, fie, foe, fum, 5
First I loosen mud and dirt, 19
Five fingers on this hand, 11
Five little ants in an ant hill, 63
Five little chickadees sitting on the floor, 60
Five little ducks went in for a swim, 36
Five little froggies sat on the shore, 62

Five little girls woke up in their beds, 20
Five little Indians running through a door, 61
Five little jack-o'-lanterns sitting on a gate, 95
Five little kittens standing in a row, 64
Five little snow men standing in a row, 48
Five little soldiers standing in a row, 66

Going to the circus to have a lot of fun, 100
Golden fishes swimming, floating, 35
Good little mother, how do you do?, 40
Good morning now we'll say, 80
Good morning to you, Valentine, 99

Hands on shoulders, hands on knees, 13
Hear the merry Christmas bells, 92
Here are Grandma's spectacles, 41
Here are two telegraph poles, 66
Here is a bunny with ears so funny, 36
Here is the chimney, 94
Here is the church, 52
Here stands a lovely Christmas tree, 93
Here we go up, up, up, 76
Here's a cup, and here's a cup, 83
Here's a great big hill, 23
Here's a little wash bench, 83
Hickory, dickory, dock, 31
Hold on tightly as we go, 77
Hot cross buns, 66

I am a fine musician, 87
I am the witch's cat, 96
I have a little watch right here, 27
I have a top, 27
I have ten little fingers, 3

I saw a little bird go hop, hop, hop, 37
I shut the door and locked it tight, 81
I think when a little chicken drinks, 36
If I had an airplane, 22
If I were a witch, 98
If I'd put a feather in my hat, 17
I'm a friendly ghost—almost, 97
I'm a little teapot, short and stout, 82
I'm three years old and like to wear, 17
I've a jack-o'-lantern, 95

Jack and Jill went up the hill, 52
Jack-in-the-box, all shut up tight, 55
Johnny works with one hammer, 67

Kitty, kitty, kitty, kitty, 42
Knock at the door, 13

Leg over leg, 30
Let your hands clap, clap, clap, 90
Let's drive our auto down the street, 25
Little Jack Horner, 94
Little Robin Redbreast, 37

Many leaves are falling down, 47
Mister Thumb, Mister Thumb, where are
    you?, 5
"My bunnies now must go to bed," 43
My fingers are so sleepy, 43
My hands upon my head I place, 12
My hat, it has three corners, 17
My rabbit has two big ears, 34
My zipper suit is bunny brown, 18

Old shoes, new shoes, 18
Once I saw a bunny, 35
One for the money, 70
One little, two little, three little Indians, 69
One little, two little, three little witches, 95
One silk, two silk, three silk, zan, 74
One, I see, 70
One, two, buckle my shoe, 66
One, two, three, four, five; I caught a hare
    alive, 64
One, two, three, four, five, I caught a little
    fish alive, 60
One, two, three, four, five little frogs, 62

One, two, three, four, five little squirrels, 63
One, two, three, four, five, six, seven, all good
    children, 71
One, two, three, four, Mary at the cottage
    door, 74
One, two, three little chickens, 42
Open, close them; open, close them, 79

Pat-a-cake, pat-a-cake, baker's man, 80
Peas porridge hot, 88
Pitter-pat, pitter-pat, 46
Please, everybody, look at me, 101
Point to the right of me, 11
Poor old Jonathan Bing, 56
Pound pound goes the hammer, 89

Rain is falling down, 47
Rock-a-bye baby on the tree top, 52
Rock-a-bye baby, thy cradle is green, 44
Row, row, row your boat, 26

Said this little fairy, 57
See my big and scary eyes, 97
See my pumpkin round and fat, 97
See the little mousie, 30
See the window I have here, 78
Shake, shake, knock, knock, 88
Sing a song of sixpence, 55
Slide your fingers into the wide part, 18
Snip, snip, snip, snippety, 57
Snip, snip, snip the paper, 99
Snowflakes whirling all around, 48

Tap at the door, 81
Ten little firemen, sleeping in a row, 53
Ten little fishes were swimming in a school,
    74
Ten little grasshoppers sitting on a vine, 65
Ten little Indians standing in a row, 90
Ten little Men standing in a row, 70
Ten little soldiers standing in a row, 88
The alligator likes to swim, 32
The bear went over the mountain, 34
The famous King of France, 53
The finger band is coming to town, 86
The fish lives in the brook, 81

The great big train goes up the track, 22
The Indians are creeping, 57
The leaves are dropping from the trees, 47
The little leaves are whirling round, 47
The month is October, 47
The seesaw goes up, 78
The snail is so slow, 37
The steam shovel scoop opens its mouth so wide, 26
The wheels of the bus go round and round, 25
The windshield wipers on our car, 24
There was a great big stilt man, 50
There was a little turtle, 33
There was a man lived in the moon, 51
They do so, so, so, 4
Thieken man, build the barn, 57
This is a choo-choo train, 23
This is a very nice jack-o'-lantern, 97
This is little Tommy Thumb, 4
This is my father, 41
This is my garden, 46
This is my right hand, 9
This is my turtle, 32
This is the circle that is my head, 14
This is the mother, kind and dear, 41
This is the roof of the house so good, 76
This is the way, all the long day, 26
This is the way my fingers stand, 3

This is the way we blow our balloon, 89
This is the way we wash our shirt, 84
This little calf eats grass, 38
This little doggie ran away to play, 30
This little fellow is ready for bed, 101
This little girl does nothing but play, 82
This little pig went to market, 32
This little squirrel said, "Let's run and play," 35
This old man, he played one, 68
"Thumb in the thumb place . . . ," 20
Thumbkin, Pointer, Middleman big, 4
Thumbkin says, "I'll dance," 8
Tick, tick, tick, tick, says the metronome, 28
Two little blackbirds sitting on a hill, 73
Two little ducks that I once knew, 71
Two little hands so soft and white, 12
Two little houses closed up tight, 70
Two mother pigs lived in a pen, 72

Up a step, and up a step, 79
Up the steps we will go, 78

Warm hands, warm, 55
Way up in the apple tree, 48
When it's cold, you shiver and you quiver, 58
Where is Thumbkin?, 6
Who feels happy, who feels gay?, 76
Wind, wind, wind the bobbin, 78

Index of Titles

Aiken Drum, 51
Airplane, An, 22
Alligator, The, 32
Apples, 48
Auto, Auto, 24

Balloons, 89
Bear Went over the Mountain, The, 34
Bedtime, 101
Big Hill, 23
Big Train, The, 22
Boats, The, 26
Bumblebee, 73
Bunnies' Bedtime, 43
Bunny, 36
Bus, The, 25
Busy Fingers, 3

Catching a Fish, 60
Chickadees, 60
Chickens, 42
Choo-Choo Train, 92
Christmas Bells, 92
Christmas Is A-Coming, 92
Christmas Tree, 93
Circus, The, 100
Clap Your Hands, 10
Clocks, 27
Coal-Black Cat, 98
Cobbler, Cobbler, 18
Come Follow Me, 9
Counting Out, 71
Creeping Indians, 57

Dog Went to Dover, 30
Doggie's Tail, 30

Down by the Station, 22
Dressing, 16
Driving down the Street, 25

Eensy, Weensy Spider, 31
Eeny, Meeny, Miney, Mo, 73
Eye Winker, 11

Falling Leaves, 47
Family, The, 41
Feather in My Hat, 17
Fee, Fie, Foe, Fum, 5
Finger Band, The, 86
Five Fingers, 11
Five Little Ants, 63
Five Little Ducks, 36
Five Little Froggies, 62
Five Little Girls, 20
Five Little Indians, 61
Five Little Kittens, 64
Five Little Squirrels, 63
Five Years Old, 101
Friendly Ghost, The, 97
Frogs, 62

Golden Fishes, 35
Good Little Mother, 40
Good Morning, 80
Grandma's Spectacles, 41
Grasshoppers, 65
Great Big Ball, 64

Hair Ribbons, 17
Halloween Witches, 95
Hammering, 88
Hands on Shoulders, 13

Helpfulness, 82
Here Is the Chimney, 94
Here Is the Church, 52
Here's a Cup, 83
Hickory, Dickory, Dock, 31
Hot Cross Buns, 66
House, The, 76

I Am a Fine Musician, 87
I Caught a Hare, 64
I Have a Little Watch, 27
I Shut the Door, 81
Indians, 90
I've a Jack-o'-Lantern, 95

Jack and Jill, 52
Jack-in-the-Box, 55
Jack-o'-Lanterns, 95
Johnny's Hammer, 67
Jonathan Bing, 56

King of France, 53
Kitten Is Hiding, 32
Kitty, Kitty, 42
Knock at the Door, 13

Leaves, 47
Let Your Hands Clap, 90
Little Bird, 37
Little Fingers, 4
Little Jack Horner, 94
Little Mousie, 30
Little Robin Redbreast, 37
Little Wash Bench, The, 83

Make a Valentine, 99
Mary at the Cottage Door, 74
Metronome Song, The, 28
Mister Thumb, 5
Mittens, 18
Mitten Song, The, 20
My Garden, 46
My Hands, 12
My Hat, 17
My Pumpkin, 97
My Rabbit, 34

My Turtle, 32
My Zipper Suit, 18

October, 47
Old Shoes, New Shoes, 18
Once I Saw a Bunny, 35
One for the Money, 70
One, Two, Buckle My Shoe, 66
Open, Close Them, 79
Our Table, 94

Pat-a-Cake, 80
Peas Porridge, 88
People, 50
Pitter-Pat, 46
Playmates, 54
Point to the Right, 11
Pound Goes the Hammer, 89

Raindrops, 47
Right Hand, Left Hand, 9
Rock-a-Bye Baby, 52
Rock-a-Bye Baby, Thy Cradle Is Green, 44
Row, Row, Row Your Boat, 26

Said This Little Fairy, 57
Santa Claus, 92
Scary Eyes, 97
Seesaw, The, 78
Shake, Shake, Knock, Knock, 88
Shiny Shoes, 19
Shiver and Shake, 58
Sing a Song of Sixpence, 55
Sleepy Fingers, 43
Snail Song, 37
Snip, Snip, Snip, Snippety, 57
Snowflakes, 48
Snow Men, 48
Soldiers, 66
Steam Shovel, The, 26
Stilt Man, The, 50
Swinging, 77

Tap at the Door, 81
Teapot, The, 82
Tee-Taw-Buck, 74

Telegraph Poles, 66
Ten Fingers, 3
Ten Little Firemen, 53
Ten Little Fishes, 74
Ten Little Indians, 69
Ten Little Men, 70
Ten Little Soldiers, 88
Tennessee, 70
There Was a Little Turtle, 33
Thieken Man, 57
This Is the Circle That Is My Head, 14
This Is the Mother, 41
This Little Calf, 38
This Little Doggie, 30
This Little Pig, 32
This Little Squirrel, 35
This Old Man, 68
Thumbkin, Pointer, 4
Thumbkin Says, "I'll Dance," 8
Tommy Thumb, 4
Top, The, 27
Train, The, 22
Two Little Blackbirds, 73
Two Little Ducks, 71

Two Little Hands, 12
Two Little Houses, 70
Two Mother Pigs, 72

Up a Step, 79
Up the Steps We Go, 78
Up, Up, 76

Valentine for You, 99
Valentine's Good Morning, 99
Very Nice Jack-o'-Lantern, 95
Very Nicest Place, The, 81

Warm Hands, 55
We Wash Our Shirt, 84
When a Little Chicken Drinks, 36
Where Is Thumbkin?, 6
Whirling Leaves, 47
Who Feels Happy?, 76
Wind the Bobbin, 78
Window, The, 98
Windshield Wipers, The, 24
Witch, 98
Witch's Cat, 96